PALMISTRY SECRETS REVEALED

The Arabs say that when a child is born his destiny is written upon his forehead. According to palmists, a person's fate and character are not only prewritten but are visible in the markings of his hands and in the shape of both fingers and hands.

If you are intrigued by the lines in your palm, want to know the length of your life line, what your health line is and whether it bodes well for you, this book will be your guide.

The author is one of Britain's foremost palmists. He explains simply and clearly for beginners and more advanced readers what each line means in relation to other factors. Just one reading of the book should enable you to read your own palm! Further thorough study of these instructions will equip you to read other people's hands, tell them the inner meanings of their palm lines, their characters, their past histories, and their futures!

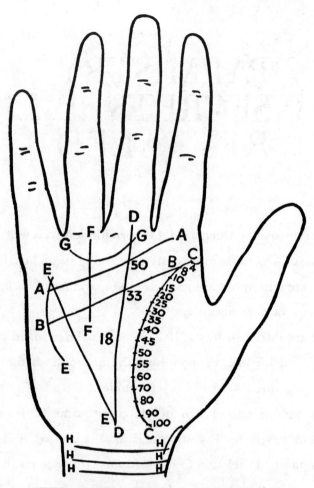

THE HAND AND ITS MARKINGS

EXPLANATION OF DIAGRAM

AA Line of Heart
BB Line of Head
CC Line of Life
DD Line of Fate

EE Line of Health
FF Line of Apollo
GG Girdle of Venus
HH The Rascettes

PALMISTRY SECRETS REVEALED

HENRY FRITH

Edited by John Malcolm

Published by
Melvin Powers
WILSHIRE BOOK COMPANY
12015 Sherman Road
No. Hollywood, California 91605
Telephone: (213) 875-1711 / (818) 983-1105

Printed by

HAL LEIGHTON PRINTING COMPANY
P.O. Box 3952
North Hollywood, California 91605
Telephone: (213) 983-1105

ISBN 0-87980-116-6

Manufactured in the United States of America

CONTENTS

INTRODUCTION

PALMISTRY is one of the oldest and most engaging of all studies. It has survived over thousands of years, from the days of the ancient Hindus and Greeks, when it played a great role in their religion and philosophy, to the present day. During this time it has been proved over and over again that certain marks on the hands, in conjunction with other related signs, do very definitely indicate certain events in a person's past, present and/or future history.

The lines in the hands do not appear by accident, neither are they made by constant folding of the hand; each mark or line has a meaning and significance for the individual. It has been found that there are natural positions in the hand for certain lines, such as the Life and Heart lines, and any deviation from these natural positions has some special significance.

Every emotional experience which a person undergoes is marked on the hands, so that over a period of years the lines of the hands change. Marks appear where before there were none and lines which before were distinct may perhaps become less so.

In this book we have tried to describe, as simply as possible, the recognized meanings of the most commonly found marks and lines on the hand, and hope that we shall succeed in interesting you in this really fascinating and age-long subject.

CHAPTER I

The Seven Types of Hands

WE SHALL START by describing in detail the different types of hands, of which seven are recognized in Palmistry. They can be distinguished by the shapes and general appearance of the fingers and thumbs and are classified as follows:—

1. The Spatulate.
2. The Square.
3. The Artistic or Conic.
4. The Elementary.
5. The Mixed.
6. The Philosophic.
7. The Psychic.

You will find that all hands fall into one of these seven groups. The most common types, however, are the Spatulate, the Square and the Conic, or Artistic.

Both hands should always be studied, as the right hand carries out the indications of the left.

THE SPATULATE HAND

A hand with Spatulate finger-tips (FIG. 1) indicates a person with a dynamic personality, brimming with energy, self-reliance and constancy. It also indicates a seeker after plenty and a person with a desire to benefit himself and make himself useful. At times owners of these splay-tips are annoying, as they must be doing something and the owners are inclined to worry. A woman with such fingers and a big thumb will always be tidying-up. A person with these hands will have no taste for literature or art.

These are the obvious indications of the Spatulate tips. Now look at the fingers below the nails.

Are they smooth or knotted? Are the joints developed or not? Let us take the smooth variety first.

The smoothness of the fingers indicates a slight inclination towards art and ease; but though people with fingers of this type may appreciate art, they will not themselves be artists. They will like to have the beautiful and elegant in their houses and they will also like comfort. They will be active, too, and will not mind working with their hands. If the fingers are long as well as smooth, the owners will be fond of useful work such as gardening and, perhaps, farming. Such fingers indicate activity of mind and body, enjoyment of sports such as riding, shooting, cricket and so on, a fondness for music and possibly an ability to play a musical instrument, but no singing talent.

If the fingers are short, the owner is one to make quick impressions. He will ignore details and accept only the " mass." Spatulated fingers denote a man or woman fitted to build up a colony, because they are not afraid of work, have little sentiment and are fond of tilling, sowing, ploughing and all real actions. Being self-reliant they are generally able to rough it, as their appetites and passions are not greatly in evidence and they can dispense with luxury.

If the Spatulate fingers are knotted—that is, well developed at the joints—great order is indicated. Here is a person with an active and very practical mind and no sentiment. Sometimes there is a lack of consideration and a certain roughness of speech, but fingers of this type carry with them talents for engineering and inven-

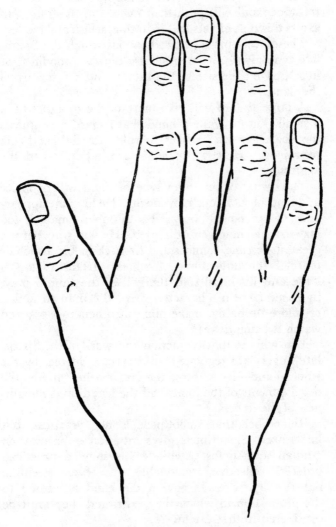

FIG. I. The Spatulate Hand.

tions.   They show aggressiveness, perseverance and resistance and will push their owners to the front.   In excess this type of person is irritating, selfish and tactless.

These are some of the indications which the Spatulate type gives us, but of course they are modified or increased by the size of the thumb and the texture of the hand.

A large thumb will give more of the qualities than a small thumb, while a hand that is hard accentuates the character who wishes to rule and dislikes being restrained.   Here we have the revolutionist and the aggressor.

The owner of the softer type of hand will be lazier and fond of vicarious movement.   He likes the appearance of movement, but, if his thumb is small, is too lazy to make much effort himself.   He will travel in the greatest possible comfort and sit back in his armchair to read the adventures of others.   If his thumb is large and his hand soft, the will of the thumb may, by sheer force of character, drive the man to action or, more probably, make him put others to work and watch it being done!

You will see that the action and work of the Spatulate fingers are regulated, to a certain degree, by the whole hand—its texture, the size of the thumb, the developments of the joints and the length and smoothness of the fingers.

Remember that smoothness is not practical, but knots are.   Smoothness gives intuition or inspiration and an artistic taste, while knots show a practical, orderly, reflective, reasonable and even scientific nature.   These traits govern the hand according to the proportion in which they exist, and they must be considered to that extent.

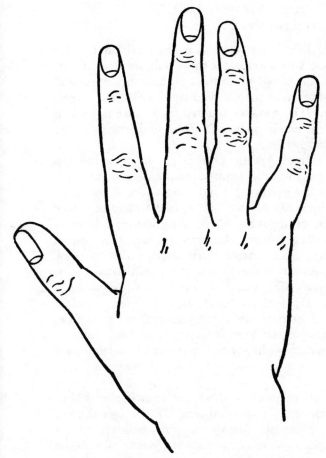

Fig. 3. The Artistic (or Conic) Hand.

type. This hand makes its owner regular and punctual at meals, tidy, polite, sympathetic, just and respectful to authority; he is not romantic.

THE ARTISTIC TYPE

The Artistic hand (FIG. 3) is the next on our list and is one which possesses the Conic form of finger. It is familiar to all of us in the hands of artists and singers—the great pianist does not have conic fingers as a rule. The conic or pointed fingers are not useful and the extremely pointed indicate uselessness and an unpractical person.

The medium Artistic form is good. The hand is supple and soft, the palm a moderate size and the thumb rather small. A hand of this sort, if the bases of the fingers are not too heavy, is the hand of a true artist. Its owner is impulsive, imaginative, a lover of the beautiful, rather self-indulgent and, because of his smooth, conic, rather thick fingers, likes to enjoy himself. As a rule this type is easily influenced by his surroundings and will pass from grave to gay in a moment. He does not like to be controlled, nor does he wish to control others. Combined with impulse, cheerfulness, carelessness, enjoyment and love of ease are a peculiar obstinacy and absence of real love, for he likes novelty and his nature is not warm for very long.

These characteristics affect the individual as they become more or less accentuated. The larger thumb, the larger palm and smoother fingers which are thicker at the bases show less order and more love of material pleasures. The small second phalange of the thumb gives tact or finesse with its weaker reason, the larger top

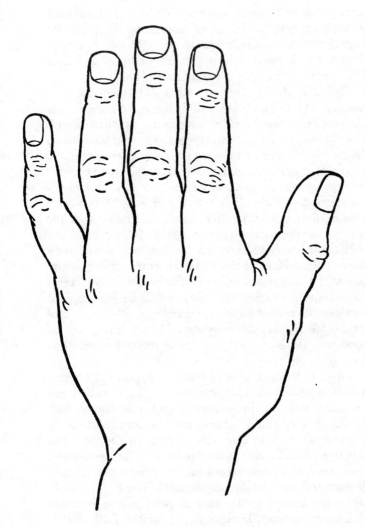

FIG. 4. The Elementary Hand.

joint more will power and the full ball of the thumb stronger passions. In these points we find all the ingredients for sensual enjoyment. The pleasures of the senses are the delight of the artistic hand and their affections are impulsive, strong and fickle.

The soft, thick, large artistic hand shows signs of finesse, cynicism, lying, shrewdness, cunning and extreme sensuality. The possessors of such hands enjoy beauty, not for any mental reason, but purely to gratify a taste. They often look effeminate and they are eccentric. They are egotists, with flyaway natures, generous to their intimate friends but close-fisted to creditors. They have an extremely warm imagination and are often *poseurs*. Venus and the Moon rule their palms.

If these hands are knotted the indications are more favourable. Here there is less eccentricity and more reason. There is still a love of the beautiful, but it is a more refined attachment; the art will be less inspired and less successful in its originality, but the love of form and beauty will be there. If the hands are of good size, thick and short, a strong desire for wealth is indicated.

There is another kind of hand with pointed fingers, which is useless and unpractical. This is called the Psychic hand and indicates the seeker of the highest beauty, purity and goodness, the best and most lovely form of the artistic instincts. Although they are not practical hands, like the Square or the Spatulate, their very real desire to win the good makes them determined and terrible opponents. These soft, small, tapering-fingered hands may be seen in the warriors of Eastern nations, fanatics dying for the faith that is in them, for what they believe is right. They are

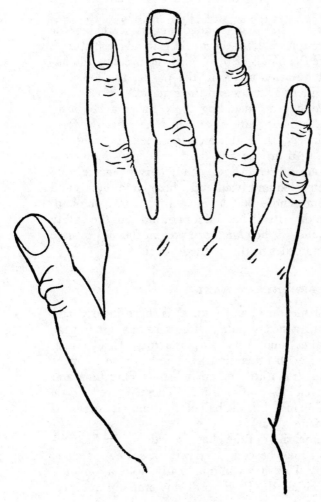

FIG. 5. The Mixed Hand.

obedient, self-sacrificing and æsthetic. But they are
completely useless for real worldly work. They are
quite unable to settle down to it. They make things,
they love beauty and are not sensual. They are
imaginative, the long, pointed fingers searching the
Universe, as it were, for the ideal the mind has pictured.
These are the hands of the vague, the dreamy, the unpractical, the non-material, the poetic, the religious,
the imprudent at times and the ecstatic.

Pointed fingers, including the conic, may be asso-
ciated with other features and in such cases the form
of the fingers, their thickness and texture, must be
weighed. An artistic and hard hand may indicate a
soldier, an officer whose characteristics make him
highly esteemed and liked and whose large thumb and
hard palm denote that he is well-fitted to command.
As a rule the artistic hand does not indicate the ability
to command. When knots are present they accentuate
reason and order in the pointed fingers.

THE ELEMENTARY HAND

The Elementary hand (FIG. 4) is short-fingered and
thick, with a heavy palm. Idiots have short fingers,
large palms and very unsatisfactory Head Lines
(combined with other signs). The common Elementary hand shows little or an indistinct Fate Line and
seems given to materialism. There is very little
imagination in it, but the ball of the thumb is developed
and the thumb thick.

Sometimes most of the characteristics of the Elementary hand may be connected with a somewhat conic
finger-tip. This shows an imaginative vein, a romantic
tinge in the mind. It will probably crop out in super-

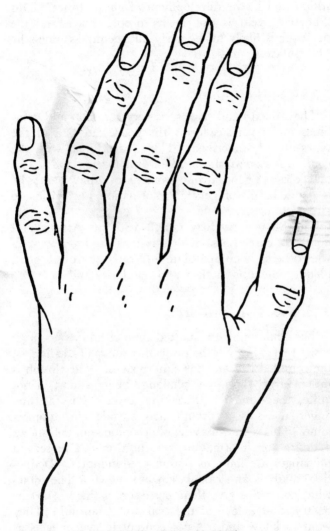

Fɪɢ. 6. The Philosophic Hand.

stition and in the development of ghost stories. This
" poetic " vein is not in its proper place and the
possessor is likely to die early and penniless unless he
finds solace in music.

THE MIXED HAND

The Mixed hand (FIG. 5) is very common and com-
bines in its various forms the good and bad of the
types already described. The square finger with the
conic tip is one form and is a diplomatic hand. The
owner is not good at one particular employment; he
is general, full of general information and yields to
circumstances.

The Elementary may mingle with the Artistic and
point to carelessness which refuses to interest itself
with others. The Spatulate and the Square is a good
blend, indicating method and regularity and so on.

THE PHILOSOPHIC HAND

The Philosophic or knotted type of hand (FIG. 6) is
easily recognized by the projecting joints of the fingers,
the rounded tips and the square sides. The thumb is
rather large, the upper phalange being almost, if not
quite, the same length as the lower. On the first
finger there is a prominence outside the topmost
joint. This is known as the philosophic knot and shows
a desire for information, an inquirer. The second
phalanges are long, as reason predominates. Deduc-
tion, analysis and calculation are shown. The somewhat conic tips give their possessors a tinge of art or
poetry, and a love of the real and beautiful. They
want to know and are not content to accept facts as

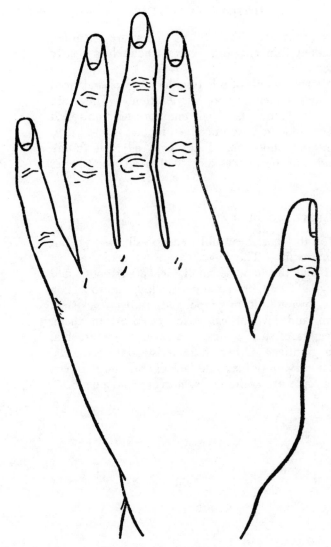

FIG. 7. The Psychic Hand.

they are; they are often cynics. They are scientific, independent thinkers, and express themselves clearly and precisely.

People with hands of this type have a well-balanced mind, independence and moderation. They are practical, not fanciful. Their emotions are controlled by reason and they are unconventional.

A knotted philosophic hand with a small thumb will indicate obstinacy and will lead the owner astray.

THE PSYCHIC TYPE

This is the most beautiful hand of all (FIG. 7), but it is not useful. The fingers are very conic, almost pointed and the hand is small, delicate, smooth and tapering. The upper phalanges are long in proportion and the lowest (also in proportion) rather thickened. Idealism and love of ease are combined in them. The owners of such hands love beauty, are ethereal and imaginative. Other characteristics are romance, love of luxury, untidiness and lack of reasoning powers. These people are enthusiastic, nervous and poetic.

CHAPTER II

The Thumb

WE HAVE DEALT at some length with the fingers
and in this chapter we are going to examine the
thumb, which is perhaps the most important of the
digits. Without the thumb we are unable to hold anything properly and the absence of this grasping power
indicates weakness or mental incapacity. Man is the
only creature to possess a thumb and this alone raises
him to the highest place in creation.

The thumb is divided into three parts in the same
way as the fingers, and these three are called, from the
nail downwards, the first and second phalange and
(the fat part) the ball of the thumb.

The three divisions, from the top downwards,
indicate the following:

1. Will-power.
2. Logic or Argument, Reasoning.
3. Love, Passion, Enjoyment.

The more developed each one of these divisions is,
the greater is the amount of the quality indicated.
Let us take them separately.

For instance, a man with a well-developed top joint
is obstinate and quarrelsome, even cruel. He is also
confident and strong-willed.

A short top-joint means change and weakness of
will, and shows an undecided person who is lacking
in self-confidence. The shorter and smaller, the less
will-power.

The second phalange should be at least as long as

the first. It is the guide to reason, judgment, thought and such qualities and should be judged with the first. It is a good sign if both upper phalanges are large.

Many people have been spoiled by the Mount of Venus, as the ball of the thumb is called. Here are found the love of music, the love of dancing, a desire to be liked and made much of, and strong passions; in other words, the sensuousness or sensuality of the subject. The warmth of the character depends to a very great extent on the development of this mount.

Any reader will be able to see the truth of these statements and make his own deductions. A small, weak top joint and a well-developed second phalange show a weak-willed, easily persuaded character, fond of amusements. He will give excellent reasons to himself and others why he should enjoy himself or laze about. He may even deceive himself if the thumb is broad and not long, for obstinacy is there.

He will argue on any topic whatsoever, having previously made up his mind on the subject, and even if his mind tells him he is possibly wrong, obstinacy will have its way and he will stick to his guns until the need for argument is withdrawn. Then he will think it over and possibly recant next time the same subject is discussed!

A thin second joint indicates impulsiveness, a lack of reasoning power but good will. It also points to some tact and judgment, if the second joint is long as well as waisted. A medium character like this has plenty of common sense and decision, but if the Mount of Venus is large the opinion of his friends will change that decision.

Even then he will be obstinate and will not yield easily to an opponent, or a person whom he dislikes.

If he is obliged to yield at last, he will lose his temper and perhaps become abusive because he has been defeated and his vanity has been hurt.

A short first phalange and a long second show a fairly reasoning, undecided character. He has quite a good imagination, but he does not carry out his ideas properly.

A thumb with a large, broad top, points to strong passion and temper, tyranny and unreasonableness. But these evils are often modified to a very great extent by some taste or calling indicated in the Mounts (see Chapter VI)—such as art or ambition—and the force may be directed towards the attainment of these ambitions.

So, before judging the thumb, look at the prime mover (Apollo, say). If Venus rules, the passions are uncontrolled, but if the Moon rules she may soothe and calm the rough will from tyrannous action or un-governable impulse to merely a hectoring manner and dictatorial tone and bearing.

The characteristics of a large Mount of Venus have been mentioned, but the smaller formations must be noticed. The medium is best, as in everything. Then affection is warm, not boiling.

If the Mount is small or entirely absent it means that the owner has a cold heart and selfish feelings. He is undemonstrative, even to his relations and to his close friends, and has no real warmth even where his own feelings are engaged.

The thumb, then, must be looked on as the key to the whole position. A small thumb—that is small from the base of the digit upwards—is a sentimental sign; here the heart rules. A large thumb rules by reason and logic.

But in judging by these rules of thumb, you must consider the softness or the hardness of the hand, the smoothness or the knottiness of the fingers, the influences of the Mounts (FIG. 8), and the length of the fingers, their thickness and their form.

A very fair opinion of the character may be given from a close inspection of the thumb, but for a true delineation it is necessary to study the whole hand and to understand the traits presented in it. I shall try to explain the general influences of these traits in later chapters.

CHAPTER III

The Fingers

SOFT HANDS mean physical laziness, but if the fingers are also square and smooth, they show a lazy mind. Soft hands also show an imaginative nature and a liking for the strange and the unseen.

Hard hands indicate energy and activity, but if they are very hard and thick they show stupidity. Selfishness and lack of intelligence are in the extremely hard hands. But hard hands can work and suffer hardships which soft ones cannot endure. Hands are not tested by the outer skin; the firmness or flexibility or softness is underneath this and can be felt by exerting gentle pressure.

Smooth fingers are those whose joints are un-developed. Knotted fingers are orderly and philo-sophic, but why this should be so is a debatable question. There must be some reason for the dif-ference and the consequent characteristics of each type, but I am afraid I am unable to give it.

The smooth finger shows a taste for art and impulse in arriving at a conclusion. Women generally have smooth fingers, or at any rate the majority have no highly developed joints. This results in their capacity for quick judgment and " inspiration."

The knotted finger is the reasonable, calculating one. The owners of fingers with knots are orderly, but the upper and lower developments indicate different kinds of order. The upper is mental, giving order in ideas, while the lower gives material order such as outward neatness and punctuality.

If both joints are developed the quantities become more accentuated. But in a female hand, with a large thumb, the subject will be worrying, and if the fingers in the same hands are long she will become fussy through the combination of love of order, attention to detail and the desire to have her own way.

But knotted fingers denote thought and order. The small bulge on the forefinger is known as the " knot of philosophy." A person with only the lower joint developed is punctual, tidy, particular and thoughtful for others. The absence of the upper swelling makes him rather unsettled in ideas.

If the first knot only is developed it shows order in ideas, originality, independence and artistic talent. If both knots exist in the fingers this talent dies and reason takes the place of art.

Long and short fingers show, respectively, love of detail and quick judgment. Short-fingered people are more impulsive and make quicker decisions, while people with long fingers are discursive, love elaboration and finicking detail and are inquisitive. These people are extremely tidy and, if their fingers are also spatulate, they are always busy at something.

Short and thick fingers are inclined to sensuousness and perhaps to cruelty and short knotted fingers show an active nature. Usually, short fingers despise details; they want results and are impulsive Therefore their owners are brusque and prompt, with staccato speech.

The length of the fingers is estimated in comparison with the palm. I will explain this in more detail later.

Before leaving the fingers let us look at the relative lengths of the phalanges. The upper phalange shows intellect, art or religion, the second reason and thought, and the third worldliness, sensuality and love of material things. Crooked fingers indicate bad instincts.

If the fingers bend backwards cunning and self-deception are indicated. A thumb which turns back means generosity.

The index, or first finger, like the thumb and all the other fingers, comprises three grades of talent, the top one being the highest, most refined and beautiful, the second the reasonable and mathematical, and the third the worldly and material.

The first phalange of the index finger is religion and (particularly when the finger is pointed) quickness. The second phalange is ambition and the third love of ruling and pride.

If the finger itself is long it tends to pride, luxury and enjoyment. If it is fairly short it shows activity. We must also look at the finger-tip. The pointed tip means intuition and the square tip means truthfulness. The index finger is dedicated to Jupiter.

The second finger, which is dedicated to Saturn, should not be very long, or else the possessor is apt to be melancholy. (There is said to be a " murderous instinct " shown if this finger is twisted, but I have no experience of this.) It does, however, most certainly carry a tendency to morbidity, a yielding to fate, a " can't help it " kind of resignation, and indicates a weak will.

This finger may be pointed, conic or square in shape. The pointed finger gives lightness and less depression and the other shapes are accompanied by gravity, energy and activity. A long, square, Saturn finger indicates a love of animals (particularly horses) and if the third finger is the same length, or very nearly the same as the second, the possessor will enjoy gambling and racing. In this case the first phalange will not be long, because gambling is not poetic, nor artistic. In such a hand, if the first phalange is long and decided it indicates active artistic tastes such as architectural or sculpting ideas. Sadness goes with the first phalange and in a weak hand this may mean depression and even suicide. If the second phalange is long, mechanical taste, scientific or agricultural ambitions are indicated. Greed, miserly instincts and selfishness are to be seen in the long third phalange.

Remember that these lengths are relative.

Art and money are to be found in the third finger, which is dedicated to Apollo. The pointed finger is the most artistic and intuitive. The spatulate form means activity in art. This often takes the form of acting. If the finger is square, it has reason in it.

The phalanges follow the tendency of the finger: art, industry, vanity and wealth, in turn. If the finger is shorter than the index finger, the owner will not be the dominant partner in marriage or business. If it is the same length as the first, it shows love of art and a wish to shine in it. This desire may also exist in the third phalange. If this finger is higher than the first, success is indicated.

The fourth finger is dedicated to Mercury. It is especially useful to business men, but it betrays the cheat, the liar and the thief, or the person who has any tendency in those directions.

If the finger is long, it indicates a person with a thirst for knowledge—scientific knowledge, in a good hand. In a bad hand this knowledge will be turned to bad uses such as business cunning and finesse. If the finger is short, the mind works quickly. If it does not rise above the top joint of the third finger the possessor will be ruled rather than ruling.

Business aptitude lies in the first phalange if the finger-tip is squared. If it is pointed, eloquence is there. The second phalange is that of the thinker, the business man and the teacher. The third phalange means industry and work, but if it is too long it shows a lying, deceitful nature. A love of writing is shown if the top joint of this finger is rather swollen.

Therefore the short fourth finger possesses quickness and intelligence and the longer finger deductive reasoning and knowledge. The pointed little finger shows the ability to talk eloquently and intuitively on any subject.

We will close this chapter with a few general remarks on the hand.

A white hand means coldness and egoism.

A hard hand means activity, and a soft one indolence.

Hairy hands show the desire for luxury and if there is hair on the phalanges anger and even cruelty is indicated. A complete lack of hair shows weakness and effeminacy.

CHAPTER IV

The Nails

THERE ARE no surer indications of character than nails, and it is odd that they have not been more fully treated in books. To look at a person's nails is a useful way of confirming one's theories. It is particularly useful as a test for temper. There may be slight variations on the following types, but the general character can be estimated from them pretty accurately.

In estimating character from the nails, the pinker part only need be considered, although the reasons for nails which are long or short beyond the finger-tips which they shield should be noticed. For instance, a bitten nail indicates nervousness and an irritable, worried temperament. Long, curving nails indicate bad tempers, particularly if they are flat instead of rounded at the bottom parts. If they are thin and fluted, they show warning signs of bad health.

Short nails—that is, nails short between the skin and the finger-tip, with a tendency in the skin to cover them—show a critical nature and often go with square fingers. If they are short, squared and wide, they indicate obstinacy. If they are short, square and long, they indicate pugnacity. Sometimes the middle finger has these characteristics, while the others are either what is known as almond-shaped, or curved at the bottom, with the thumb showing a white crescent.

In a hand with fingers like these, we may find obstinacy, irritability, kindness of heart and sensitiveness. The character is mixed and can be accurately completed by the lines of the palm.

Usually, short nails, like short fingers, denote quickness, curiosity and intuition. If the hand is lazy or easy-going, they mean a frivolous disposition. Neat, polished, well-shaped and well-cared-for nails of medium length show much delicacy of mind and good taste. If they are white, the subject is rather cold and has a high moral sense. If the nails are thin, they indicate cunning. Dark nails point to treachery and falsehood, while round nails point to luxury. White spots are generally favourable and black spots are generally unfavourable, showing loss of money or character. Brittle and splitting nails indicate delicate health.

In all cases, when the nails are short we may assume a critical, quizzing, teasing mind, which may develop, through the lines and mounts, into an intolerable worry and a quarrelsome, irritable disposition.

Pale, long or curved nails are bad signs. These point to the hard-hearted, unsympathetic man or woman who, although possibly pleasant mannered, is at times harsh and cruel.

CHAPTER V

The Palm of the Hand

WE HAVE CONSIDERED the hardness and softness of the hands, but there are a few points in connection with the palm which must be noted.

The palm of the hand should be fairly wide. In this case it indicates a broad-minded nature, intelligent and always generous-minded. To be as near perfection as possible, the palm and the fingers should be the same length. This is a good trait and a large, well-proportioned hand indicates much enjoyment in life.

A narrow, skinny hand is not a good hand to possess. It shows rather a weak mind and a lazy disposition. It is cramped, and therefore the energies are cramped too.

A palm and fingers which are even in length indicate toleration, a balance of mind and a sense of justice. The possessor can make allowances and admit his own faults.

If the palm is too hard, a proper use of the pleasures of life will degenerate into selfish enjoyment and abuse of pleasure. Even generosity will be tainted by selfishness.

A very greatly developed hand with high mounts indicates a sensual or sensuous nature. This tendency will be the same whether the hands are soft or hard, but in soft hands selfish indulgence can be seen.

The centre of the palm, which is called the " hollow of the hand," should not be too hollow, because a very deep " pond " in the palm is unlucky. A person with a palm like this will struggle, perhaps, but his efforts will often be in vain. This formation is often found in the mixed hand where energy and will may exist together, but softness may bring laziness, or too wide a palm may divert the path from worldly success. It is possible that the person may be successful in love or gain his end in amusement, but success in business or art will be uncertain, erratic and when it comes it will not last.

So you see that the properly regulated formation is not only correct, it is necessary. The thumbs and fingers will modify, but will not destroy the influence of the person.

CHAPTER VI

The Mounts

BEFORE we go on to the lines of the palm, let us look at the Mounts. There are not so many of them, and they are not so complicated as the lines.

The Mounts are the soft but firm swellings you will see on the palm side of the hand, at the base of the fingers and thumb (FIG. 8). Each Mount has a special significance in itself and in co-relation with the others.

THE MOUNT OF VENUS

The Mount of Venus (FIG. 8) is situated at the base of the thumb and gives us many benefits which, if wisely used and controlled, will make us happy and appreciated in the world. This Mount gives us a love for the opposite sex and admiration for it and for beauty in all forms. It gives a liking for dancing, a love of music, grace and a strong desire to please our friends and to be liked ourselves.

This Mount also belongs to the passionate lover and the flirt. But if the will is strong and pride is developed, the evil or flippant tendencies will be ruled out, even if the Mount is large.

The absence of this Mount is worse than its appearance. It shows a cold nature and a brain that is not responsive to the artistic side of life. When there is no Mount, love is absent, or selfishness creeps into the life and dims the vision and perceptions.

A very large Mount is bad and shows a passionately affectionate but inconsistent and changing nature.

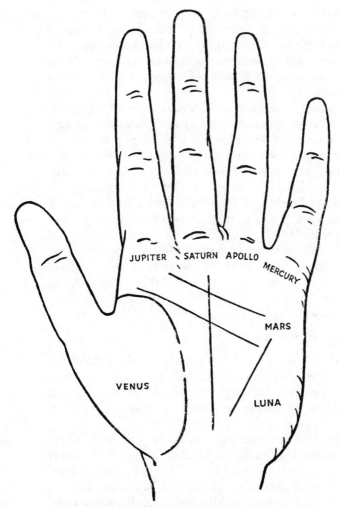

JUPITER SATURN APOLLO MERCURY

MARS

VENUS

LUNA

FIG. 8. The Mounts of the Palm.

If, on the same hand, the Heart Line is thick, it is possible that the emotions are not kept in check and the owner may be expected to fall. If the Mount of Venus is high and barred and the hand sensuous, with soft and pointed fingers, the weak will may bring about an unpleasant state of affairs, if there are no redeeming qualities.

However, the Mount of Venus gives cheerfulness, gaiety, an airy manner, liveliness with the opposite sex, a taste for feminine beauty (in a man) and a liking for the society of young people. It also gives a kindness and unselfishness and an ability to make friends easily. The Mount of Venus helps people to climb the ladders of friendship and affection, but it does not help them in their careers or their progress in the world.

The flat, crossed and barred Mount of Venus shows a very exhausted lover of pleasure and, if certain other signs are present, a person who is undesirable for a friend.

THE MOUNT OF JUPITER

The Mount of Jupiter is situated at the base of the first finger and when it is well developed it shows pride, ambition, religion, a desire to shine in society or with one's friends, a love of display and even of high religious ritual.

Jupiter is domineering and so he will want to be heard—the loud talker is ruled by Jupiter. He wants to shine in the conversation and is very self-confident. This type of person is usually tall, erect and soldier-like, slightly defiant or disdainful, and with a good opinion of himself. These attributes will be confirmed by the rather hard hand. The soft or smooth type of hand shows a love of luxury.

It is easy to see the results of an over-large Mount of Jupiter. Pride will become arrogance, domination will change to tyranny and the wish to shine will become ostentation. With this very large Mount and hard hands we find selfishness in enjoyment, and although there is a certain generosity it is of a kind which always seems to bring a response of an advantageous kind to the donor. This is particularly the case when the hands are white or the palm narrower than usual.

The results of the absence of the Mount of Jupiter are carelessness in religion, selfishness, laziness and bad manners. There is a desire to be king of the company, a certain lack of dignity and sometimes of self-respect. There is also a disregard for the feelings of others in lack of punctuality or in arrangements which affect both parties. Such a person would not mind if he kept people waiting while going on with his own amusements or interests. He would not put himself out for anyone unless he could see some advantage for himself by so doing.

THE MOUNT OF SATURN

The Mount of Saturn can be found at the base of the second finger. It is a very important Mount, because it is here that the fate of the person is developed and this melancholy Mount has the power to change our apparent destinies.

The Mount of Saturn shows a somewhat timid disposition, a love of solitude and a nature that is insensitive to criticism.

You will hardly ever find a really highly developed Mount of Saturn. It may be well developed, but tending to Apollo (the third finger) or to Jupiter, which has already been described. But in cases where Saturn is truly developed we may find a morbid tendency to melancholy, suicide, unreasonable fears and sadness.

It is, however, a comforting thought that this Mount is so seldom highly developed. This tends to confirm the fact that one's own fate is very greatly dependent on one's own conduct.

A small Mount and a good Fate Line are indications of success. Prudence is a characteristic and this will enable the person to be successful, if his hand is otherwise favourable. The position of the Mount, in relation to those beside it, will help to decide this.

THE MOUNT OF APOLLO

The Mount of Apollo lies at the base of the third finger and indicates a sunny temperament and a pleasant personality. It is in this Mount that we find art, literature, artistic tastes and a charitable disposition. The truest and best qualities of our nature lie in this Mount, together with some of those failings which are somehow almost inseparable from the artistic temperament, such as carelessness, fickleness and a sensitiveness which often breaks up a friendship.

The well-developed Mount of Apollo loves art and beauty for their own sakes. In this case the hand will not be sensual. The fingers may be smooth, with the carelessness and lack of order which characterize those devoted to art. True artists like this will not pose in public. They want to shine, but in sympathetic surroundings. The executive artist will have conic or useful finger-tips and fairly long fingers.

In excess this Mount leads us astray. It indicates extravagance, exaggeration, luxury and boastfulness. This hand will have a sensual type of finger, indicating activity, ardour and little calculation. The hand will be soft and the possessor will be full of self-importance, while all the time he is unstable, frivolous, false and envious. (Both hands should be consulted.)

The absence of any Mount of Apollo is a bad sign, especially if there is no Mount of Saturn and no lines in the place of Apollo. Lack of sun kills us in time and so the absence of its Mount in our hand indicates an aimless kind of existence, an insignificant life and a liking for low pleasures.

Lines on this Mount, as on all the others, have a certain significance, which we shall consider fully later.

Even if there are no lines on the Mount, the liking for and the appreciation of art is still there and also a desire for artistic production.

THE MOUNT OF MERCURY

The Mount of Mercury is found at the base of the fourth finger. As its name implies, it gives quickness, smartness, intelligence, wit, invention and aptitude for business.

It also indicates the power of expression, a quick mind and the ability to write.

All these are contained in Mercury, the lively spirit which wants change of scene, the intelligence to appreciate it and the eloquence to describe it in a true and imaginative way.

If this Mount is very highly developed the business aptitude becomes too great, the smartness becomes dishonesty, invention turns to lying, and the promptness to take an advantage becomes robbery and treachery. The self-deceiving fingers (those that are turned back) excuse many things and the soft hands mean laziness—a desire to gain anyhow and to spend the gains extravagantly.

The total absence of this Mount denotes failure in business and a negative, aimless existence.

The possessors of the mercurial temperament are well known. They are active and good at games and cards and are very astute. In the normal Mercurial hand the inclinations are moral. They marry early in life, sometimes purely as a business arrangement.

The Mercurial person does not spare himself either in business or in sport and does his best in both directions.

THE MOUNT OF MARS

The Mount of Mars lies a little below the Mount of Mercury and above that of the Moon (see FIG. 8). Some people say that there are two Mounts of Mars, the other one being beneath Jupiter and with functions similar to those of Jupiter. Personally, I think that only one Mount of Mars is developed in our palms and that the other apparent swelling is only an extension of Jupiter which is made rather obvious by the hollowness of the palm. But Jupiter and Mars together are successful, because ambition, devotion and courage are combined.

In the Mount of Mars, as its name implies, we find physical and moral courage, bravery and an inclina-

tion for army life. Even without Jupiter calm, cool
courage is there, resigned will, resolution and self-
respect, ease in obeying, when necessary, and the
capability to command.

The excess of Mars is not always bad. In fact at
times it may lead to success, for in the excess of courage
and gratitude there is much dash and rash bravery
which is, however, probably successful, with strength
of mind.

But the excess of Mars is not so pleasant in a hand
whose lines are bad and whose fingers are cruel.
The strength and spirit of command change to the
tyrant and the bully. A man with this excessive
development in his " bad " hand would probably
have a sadistic nature.

The absence of the Mount of Mars shows timidity,
nervousness and little presence of mind. Sometimes
one may see real cowardice here, but in many cases
pride under Jupiter will interfere and prevent any show
of cowardice, although nervous apprehension is quite
likely to appear in the same character. In this case
the Mount of Jupiter will be partly developed low
down, near the base, because the qualities of active
courage rise from the ambition and resolution of
Jupiter. The best qualities of the virtue of courage
are indicated on the Mount of Mars proper, under
Mercury.

Sometimes the Mount of Mars is absent in the left
hand, but developed in the right. (This may also be
the case with other Mounts.) The non-development
in the left hand shows that the person is naturally
nervous, timid and shy, but the development in the
right hand shows that he has some courage, although
he is of a retiring disposition. He is morally brave

and plucky in emergencies, but shrinks from putting himself forward. Where he chooses to assert himself, he leads.

THE MOUNT OF LUNA

The Mount of Luna, more commonly known as the Mount of the Moon, is situated opposite Venus (see FIG. 8) and both Mounts are often developed in the same hands.

When the Moon is well developed, it indicates romance and imagination, the poetic instinct, the observation of Nature, study of the weather, admiration of beautiful scenery and of all Nature's beauties. It also shows a love of the sea. This does not necessarily mean a love of sailing, but a love of the sea itself. With a high Mount of Venus sentimentality will also be there, but imagination, voyaging and feeling belong to the Moon.

Absence of this Mount shows little sympathy and a just but somewhat hard nature. The person cannot, without a great deal of difficulty, put himself in your place, and so his decisions will be business-like and bigoted.

In excess, the Moon is bad. It makes one dull, sad and foreboding. It indicates capriciousness, inconstancy, dissatisfaction and extreme superstition. The sentiment and the love of harmony have gone and the mind is weakened by other influences which give too strong a mixture of the moon.

So the Mounts should be studied. Once you have grasped the meanings of the Mounts, you should connect them with the presence or absence of other

Mounts, which will confirm or mitigate the influence suggested.

In this way the bad influence of Saturn may come to nothing when it is opposed by the cheerfulness of Mercury, the courage and resignation of Mars, or the love of Venus. Jupiter and Venus are good, if together. The Moon and Venus together give romantic temperaments and some beauty of form and features. Mars and Venus bring jealousy, passion and love. Apollo and Venus together bring brilliancy, fascination and charm.

According to the older accepted theories, the excess of the Mounts indicates some ill-effects on the parts of the body governed by the respective planets. Venus and the Moon rule over the lower parts of the body, Jupiter governs the head and lungs, Mars the head and throat, the Sun the heart, eyes and arms and Mercury the liver and lower limbs. Therefore, a person with an excess of Mars may have to fear illnesses affecting the throat and head, such as scarlet fever, neuralgia, or diphtheria.

But if Mars and Mercury are both in excess, indigestion and rheumatism are probable. The lines of the hand will, of course, have to be consulted for confirmation.

So illnesses would probably arise in the life of a person ruled by Mars and Mercury, but if Jupiter should come up, his power might interfere and save the person from an early death.

We will suppose that, as well as Mercury and Mars, Venus is highly developed in the hand. Strong passions are indicated, which may be too freely indulged in despite the indications of cheerfulness and courage. With a highly developed Mount of the

Moon, such indulgence will cause remorse and also depression in anticipation of detection and punishment. Saturn governs the spleen and will make the person irritable.

The person who, without Mars or Jupiter, is devoted to Venus, the Moon and Mercury, will be a sensualist without balance or courage. He will stop at nothing to gain his ends, and if Mars is added he will show talent and courage in his dissipations that are worthy of a better cause.

CHAPTER VII

Other Aspects of the Palm

THE PLAIN OF MARS is in the middle of the palm and occupies part of the hollow of the hand. If this hollow is deeper than usual, it is a sure indication that the well-meant efforts of the owner will not meet with much success. He may have luck and his perseverance and ability may give him a certain amount of success, but it will be checked and chequered. If the left hand only is hollowed, the chances of success are much greater.

The Plain of Mars lies in this hollow, just beyond the Mount of Mars. In its higher development it possesses some of the qualities of the Mount of Mars, such as perseverance and a pushing, rather aggressive temperament. If it is low, it points to a quiet, peacefully-minded disposition, which dislikes strife and quarrel. But if in the same hand the Mount of Mars is developed, the person will be aggressive with a quick temper, and when aroused will tend to fighting. A very hollow hand almost certainly shows an unsuccessful life, with no position in the chosen profession.

The Head Line (FIG. 9 B.B) crosses the Plain of Mars, and shows the life struggle which is continually going on. The Fate Line also crosses the Plain of Mars, and so our whole existence lies on the plain at one time.

The palm of the hand, like the fingers, is divided into three parts. The upper portion is the divine part, the centre the natural or reasonable, and the lowest part the material or sensual portion. The space between the Heart Line and the bases of the fingers includes the intuitive portion. The remaining zones may vary in their extent. The soft, fat hand tells its own tale—that of materialism.

On all hands spaces will be found traced on the palm, bounded by the lines. These spaces are called the Quadrangle and the Triangle. The Quadrangle lies between the Head Line and the Heart Line and the Triangle is in the Plain of Mars, bound by the Head, Health and Life Lines.

CHAPTER VIII

The Lines of the Palm

WE NOW COME to the lines of the palm of the hand. There are people who say that all lines in our palms are merely creases and that it is ridiculous to pretend to read anything in the palms of the hands. It may be true that the five main lines are natural creases in the hands of the newborn child, but it is also a fact that there are no other lines whatsoever on an infant's hands.

The other lines appear gradually, in the same way that lines appear on the face and brow.

I cannot explain why the lines are there. The hands are folded by Nature and the folding gives the crease.

Care, age, worry, illness, pain, sorrow, laughter, tears and all human emotions are at times marked on the face and brow. The habitual emotion leaves indelible traces. The nerve force may contract or expand the under surface and cause lines or furrows in the face. The same force furrows or lines our palms.

It is unfair and bigoted to recognize Physiognomy and condemn Palmistry. We judge habitually by features and faces and pride ourselves on our perception of the character we have judged in this way. But if the same character is told by the hands, the ignorant and prejudiced will in all probability say it is fortune telling.

A magistrate recently told a prisoner that if he persisted in his (then) career, he would end by penal servitude in long periods, and might possibly die by the rope. No doubt the judge made his deductions from the man's face and his record. All these traits in the man's character could undoubtedly have been read from the man's hands if the judge had known how and had cared to study them. People were quite willing to believe the judge's delineation from the face, but how many would have believed it if it had been read from the hands?

If people would only remember that the same forces probably form the lines and wrinkles on the hands at the same time that they are creating those which appear on the face, there would be far more widespread belief in Palmistry.

There are five main lines in the palm of the hand. These are:

1. The Heart Line or Mensal.
2. The Head Line or Cerebral.
3. The Life Line or Vital.
4. The Fate Line or Saturnian.
5. The Liver Line or Line of Health.

There are also the Line of Apollo or Art, the Girdle of Venus, the Quadrangle, Triangles, Line of Dissipation, the Rascettes or Bracelets, the Line of Luna and Marriage Lines. Of these the Line of Apollo comes next in importance to the first five mentioned, which we possess by the gift of Nature or because of our place in creation.

We shall consider all these lines separately and as fully as possible in relation to each other and to other signs in the hand.

From the diagram on the opposite page (FIG. 9) the position and the general direction of the chief lines can be seen.

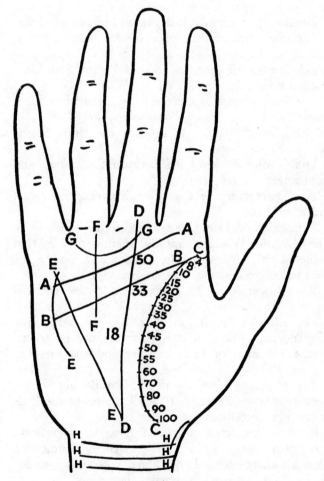

FIG. 9.   The Chief Lines of the Palm.

Compare the drawing with your own hand, but remember that the lines vary in direction.

The upper (direct) line is the Heart Line, marked A.A.

The next line below it is the Head Line, marked B.B.

The line round the thumb is the Life Line, marked C.C.

The line up the centre of the hand is the Fate Line, marked D.D.

The line sideways across the palm is the Liver Line, marked E.E.

The Line of Apollo is beneath the third finger, marked F.F.

The Girdle of Venus lies beneath the second and third fingers—G.G.

The Quadrangle is the space between the Heart and Head Lines.

The Triangles are those between the chief lines. The Grand Triangle, mostly mentioned, is that formed by the Lines of Life, Head and Liver, in the centre of the palm.

The Rascettes or Bracelets encircle the wrists—H.H.

The Line of the Moon (Luna) is not very often in evidence, but when it is there it may be traced from the Mount of Luna running towards Mercury —A.B.E.

The Marriage Lines are on the outside edge of the hand and you will see that they lie beneath the little finger, horizontally.

Each of these lines and combinations are significant and their relationships are extremely numerous. They all affect each other, adding, subtracting, multiplying and dividing amongst themselves the tendencies and influences in proportion to their respective positions. So it is of very little practical use to tell a person that his life is menaced. We must try to find the date and the cause and to verify the prediction by a reference to the other hand, before we give an opinion. Then the person, duly warned, can take care to avoid the danger. If he remembers to do so, he will probably escape and the signs of evil will disappear.

I propose to devote a whole chapter to each of the main lines of the hand and will begin with the Heart Line.

CHAPTER IX

The Heart Line

THE HEART LINE is a very important line which runs across the upper part of the hand, from near the Mount of Jupiter to the edge of the hand (see diagram, FIG. 9 A.A).

In appearance it should be well coloured, strongly marked and narrow. It should not be broken up nor rayed. Sometimes this line seems to rise or to disappear between Saturn and Jupiter. This indicates passionate affection and is also a warning that hard work will have to be done in life before the heart's desires are realized.

The appearance and continuity of the Heart Line are very important factors in our lives. If it is deep and clear and narrow, it is an indication of strong and firm affections, and of happiness. A long line is good, but it should not exceed the limits laid down above. If the line is too long, jealous and envious feelings are indicated, particularly if Venus is strong and the Head imaginative (see Luna).

A short Heart Line means a rather cold nature, though not necessarily heartless.

Many strange things can be seen on this line. It shows the state of the physical heart and the number of attachments and disappointments in the affections and their relative strength. The friendly or love attachments, if they are successful and pleasing, rise upwards from the Heart Line and indicate a person who is well liked and popular, especially with the opposite sex. These indications are not seen so often in the female hand. When they do appear, however, they are usually in the right hand, because that hand is the active one, so to speak, and shows our deeds, while the left hand merely indicates the tendencies.

If the Heart Line is chained it points to inconstancy in the affections, and when it is underlined in bands it shows some very absorbing passion. The owner of such a hand will have flirting tendencies, particularly if the line is redder than usual. Strength of passion is here and with the rayed Mount of Venus and also imagination (in Luna) it is safe to say that the subject is a general lover, unless will and pride are strong.

I have often seen marks on the Heart Line which indicate a weakness—not necessarily a disease—of the heart. I have diagnosed these marks in several cases when they have not been deep and have advised care and little violent exercise.

Once a lady who was afraid of some serious heart affection asked me my opinion concerning this mark. I told her that her heart was affected slightly, not by disease, but most probably by indigestion and that she need have no fear. However, she was not satisfied and consulted a doctor who, as she afterwards told me, confirmed my verdict in almost the same terms that I had used myself. Her fears were then allayed.

This mark is red, with a sort of indentation on the line, almost like an impression of a blunted point of a pencil.

A break in the line will denote weakness in the heart, and many breaks mean worries in the affections, out of which weakness will arise.

The total absence of a Heart Line means selfishness, great economy and an unsympathetic nature. I have actually known a case of this kind. In this person, who

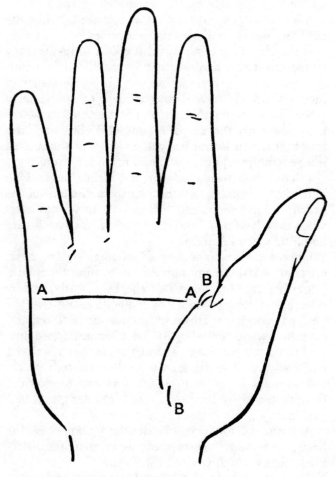

FIG. 10.

is now dead, the Heart Line was absent only from the right hand. The left hand was almost normal, but the Heart Line rose very late in the hand. The absence of the line in the right hand (FIG. 10) indicated a hard taskmaster, an economical disposition and a rather mean character. I was afterwards confirmed in this suspicion.

The hands of this person predicted a sudden failure of health. The Life Line (FIG. 11, C.C) and the Heart Line (FIG. 11, A.A) were not long where they appeared together. The Head Line (FIG. 10, A.A) in the right hand stretched stiffly across the right palm. This person was ruled by his head. He had little feeling, and yet his acquaintances found him pleasant and chatty. He could be very helpful when his earthly interests were not concerned, but where he saw his way to a bargain or a profit, no one was less sympathetic and, in money matters, more economical.

Sometimes the Heart Line goes up to Jupiter and separates. This shows that an ambition will be realized. The nearer the line is to Jupiter, the better the luck.

Lines rising clear from the Heart Line are friendships, but if the line emerges between Jupiter and Saturn unforked the person will have to work hard for his living (FIG. 11, A.A) and will never meet with any great success, unless the Line of Apollo comes to his aid. If the Heart Line ends in Jupiter, the outlook will be even less favourable.

A line without branches (which I myself have never seen) would indicate a loveless life. In this case, the Head Line would be strong.

No Heart Line in either hand is a very bad sign. If the Heart Line exists without break under the little finger, the chances are that when the person marries he will have no family. This applies both to the male and female hand.

White marks on the Heart Line denote conquests in love. I have seen such marks. But on some hands where, knowing the reputation of the people concerned, I would have expected such marks to appear, there have been none. Certainly the lines were cut and separated, indicating passion. But where there were any dots at all, they were extremely faint. This indicated that actual love had little to do with such people's regard. In some other hands there were a few white specks beneath the line. I have also seen red points in the Heart Line and consider them as trials and heart worries concerning the affections, if not physical disease.

When the Heart Line actually breaks under a certain Mount, the cause of the disappointment and trouble comes from circumstances connected with the indications of the finger. I have seen two divisions of this sort in one hand. One break occurred fairly early in life beneath the finger of Saturn (FIG. 12, 1–1), fell in the direction of the Head Line and dropped a root over it to the Life Line. The other break (FIG. 12, 2–2) occurred some time after, just under the third finger, towards the thumb side. This break sent out a well-marked line which crossed the Head Line and the Life Line and finally joined another line which ran parallel to the Life Line.

The explanation is not difficult. The Mount of Venus was well developed, and this pointed to sentiment, imagination, poetic instinct and orderliness. The fingers were square, but gently rounded, indicating a mixed type.

The breaks in the Heart Line indicated broken

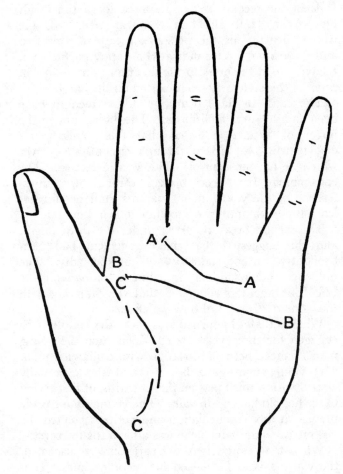

Fig. 11.

engagements which worried the person very much. Indeed, the second break interfered for a time with his career. But although the scar remained, the wound healed, for the person subsequently married and a cross on Jupiter indicated a happy partnership. I have added the cross to the diagram (FIG. 12, 3), in proof of this statement, as it existed on the hand.

The cause of these heart wounds seemed to have been fatality and foolishness. The break under the finger of Saturn indicated that the young man's engagement was broken through circumstances over which he had no control. This was in fact so. The engagement had been broken through the interference of the young man's parents, and he did not learn the truth until it was too late to mend matters.

The second break occurred under the third finger, and this suggested that the engagement had been brought to an end suddenly and unexpectedly. The influence ended suddenly in a line accompanying the Life Line and this suggested that the fault lay with the woman. It showed that *she* left *him*.

What actually happened was this: the couple were engaged for three years, after which time the young man's fiancée began a flirtation with a married man. The young man gave her up and she eventually eloped with a third person, but not without first trying to see her old fiancé—in vain. The young man's pride prevented any reconciliation and perhaps goaded the girl into a course which she was afterwards to regret.

When a weakness in the Heart Line is suspected, the cause should be looked for in other lines. It is absolutely essential to consult all the lines before coming to a conclusion, because you may be mistaken in the marks on any one line.

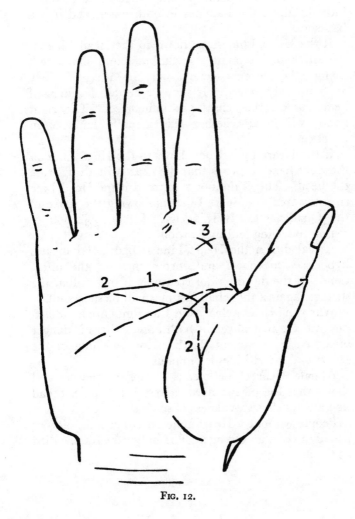

FIG. 12.

The Heart Line should not drop down to the Head Line and the Head Line should not rise to the Heart. But sometimes this happens in both hands and it is a bad sign.

If the Heart Line drops down to the Head Line on the left hand, it points to selfishness and shows that though the person's feelings may be attracted, they are not easily moved. It shows a certain hardness of heart, unless the senses are influenced. The right hand will show whether this actually happens in practice.

If the Heart Line drops down to the Head Line on the right hand it means that the heart will always rule the head. This is doubly confirmed if the Head Line rises towards the Heart Line, narrowing the space of the Quadrangle. It is a sign of the subjection of reason to feeling and inclination.

A real dip in the Heart Line is bad. It indicates hypocrisy, meanness and inconstancy in the affections. If the dip does not continue, it means that the struggle against these bad instincts will be successful.

When the Heart, Head and Life Lines are all joined beneath the first finger in both hands, there is danger of an early or violent death. Any touching of the Heart and Head Lines is ominous.

A pale Heart Line means a lack of power, and shows that the person needs a rest. The pale, broad line always shows weakness of some sort.

People without a Heart Line on either hand do not usually live to an old age. The only case I knew died at the age of 52.

CHAPTER X

The Head Line

THE HEAD LINE is another important line in the palm, and we can obtain a great deal of information from it.

It lies beneath the Heart Line and should extend across the palm from beneath the base of Jupiter, about halfway between the first finger and the thumb (see FIG. 9, B.B).

The Head Line should be joined with the Life Line for a while (see the diagram), then leave it and proceed by itself in a slightly sloping direction to the other side of the hand, perhaps falling to the Mount of the Moon or rising to Mercury, or continuing in a hard line across the hand.

A hard line, running right across the hand, shows a calculating, economical nature. It shows a man who will haggle over the price of the cheapest article, even though he intends to buy it. Where there is no Heart Line, this Head Line is bad. But by hardness and economy it brings success of a kind.

If the Head Line is even, long, and clear it indicates good judgment and a good intellect.

The broken, descending, pale line indicates weakness and irresolution.

When the Head Line leaves the Life Line early in the hand (FIG. 13, A.A), it shows self-confidence and, in extreme cases, conceit. This is a successful formation and the self-confidence enables the person to smile at and to despise criticism. He is fairly thick-skinned. A powerful thumb in a hand with this Head

Line indicates ambition and the will to succeed. In a weak hand it may mean merely impudence and a pushing personality. It indicates, too, rapid decision, which is sometimes entirely wrong (see also FIGS. 12 and 10).

When the Head Line is joined to the Life Line for some time, it indicates shyness and timidity. This shyness is often hidden under an abrupt manner.

An excess of this formation (FIG. 14, A.A) is bad for the development of the intellect. The life is not sufficiently independent and the person will require gentle treatment. His brain may be sluggish or, on the other hand, he may have too rapid a brain. On the whole I think the long-joined Head and Life Lines is an indication of a timid, undeveloped nature, but possibly clever and eccentric. White marks at the separation of the lines point to delicacy of the eyes in youth.

A long Head Line (in a rayed hand) indicates thought and coolness and readiness in case of action. The head gives substance to the ideas suggested by the many rays in the palm.

When the Head Line is entirely separated from the Life Line it shows a tendency to carelessness. If this Head Line is also a good one, and there is a good Mount of Mars, it will bring a somewhat rash bravery into the character.

The Life Line should be connected with the Head, or else the care for existence is lessened. If the Head Line is short and weak and separated from the Life Line (FIG. 13), there is jealousy as well as carelessness.

If the Head Line is strong and separated from the Life Line it indicates great confidence. If the line is long also, it points to a brusque, decided manner with

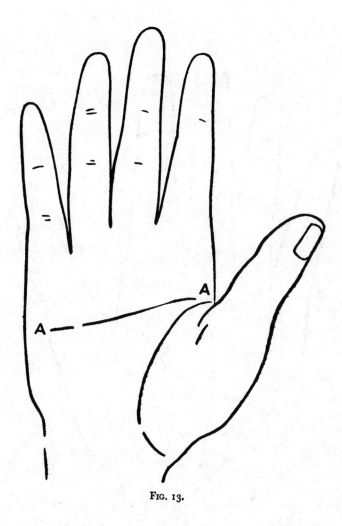

FIG. 13.

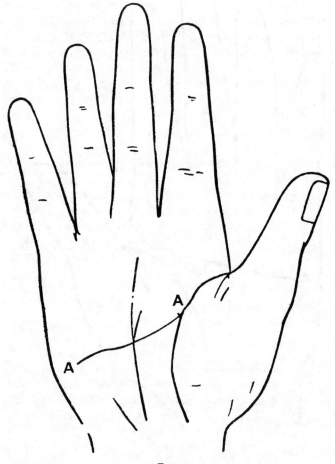

Fig. 14.

very little consideration for other people's feelings. The person often says things that hurt, simply from lack of tact.

The Head Line often curves downwards and goes into the Mount of the Moon, sometimes ending in a fork. This descending Head Line (FIG. 15, A.A) is imaginative and in many ways is not practical. It indicates idealism and a person with a happy-go-lucky nature. It is a literary and poetic kind of Head Line. If the Mount of the Moon is large and Venus is present, it shows that romance and sentiment exist. If the little finger is thick at the top joint, the owner has the ability to write.

White specks in or under the Head Line indicate literary success.

A forking Head Line similar to the one in FIG. 15, A.B, is a good sign. It points to descriptive powers that are useful in writing or in conversation. But if the upper fork ends in Mercury (FIG. 15, A.C) and the lower one sinks down, the imagination will be too well developed and will cause a deceitful nature. Finesse will become hypocrisy and with a cross-rayed Mercury it may become dishonesty and fraud.

But the simple fork in a good hand is not a drawback. It gives tact and diplomacy.

A very far descending Head Line (FIG. 15, A.D) with a break in it, or that ends in a star, together with a chained Heart Line, is a bad omen. A person with this formation may develop brain trouble. If the Head Line is broken his mind will be affected and his memory will fail.

A broken Head Line (FIG. 16, A.A) means lack of concentration and if it turns up a branch to Jupiter (FIG. 16, B.B) the person's pride will be very sensitive.

If the branches tend to Saturn (FIG. 16, C.C) a legacy or monetary success is indicated. If the branches tend to Mercury (FIG. 16, D.E) business success is likely. If the branches tend to Apollo (FIG. 16, D.D) success in art is indicated. It is quite possible for a person to have lines in Apollo and Mercury, for instance. He may have an artistic temperament or perhaps actually be an artist of some kind and also have a keen business sense.

Accidents to the head are indicated by red points, or breaks, according to their severity. I have never seen any very serious accidents predicted.

If the Head Line turns up to Saturn through the Heart Line, there is great danger of death from wounds in the head.

If the Head Line meets and joins the Heart Line the heart will always rule the head. The passions will over-rule reason.

The joining of Life, Head and Heart Lines (FIG. 17, A.A.A) is a sign of violent death, probably suicide. The Life Line must be consulted for the date of death, particularly if it ends suddenly with a bar across it (FIG. 17).

Sometimes an island appears on the Head Line (FIG. 17, B.B) (see also Chapter XIX). This island usually indicates very sensitive nerves and also neuralgia.

If the Head Line is chained it shows lack of concentration. If it is pale and rather wide a weak mind is indicated. It is a good and lucky sign if another line runs parallel to the Head Line. If one is broken, the other line will counteract the evil. A double line means that one will inherit money. All breaks in the line are bad signs.

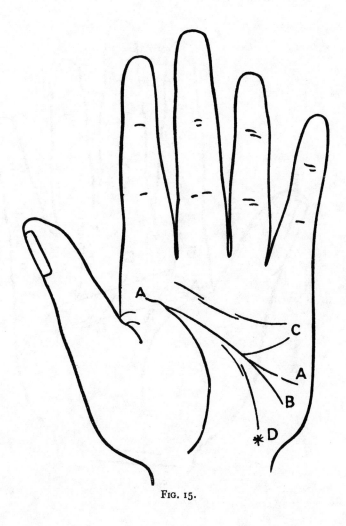

Fig. 15.

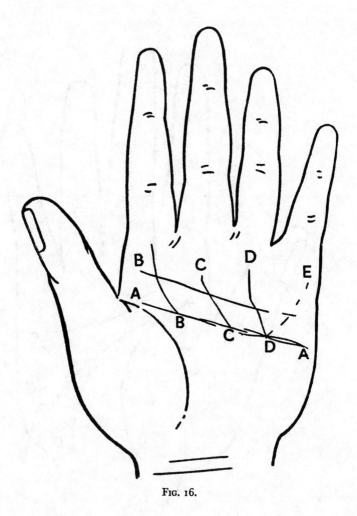

FIG. 16.

A short Head Line is also bad. . If it ends under Saturn, it indicates an early and sudden death. Compare the Life Line and the Fate Line; it is unlucky if the Head Line ends at the Fate Line in the Plain of Mars and indicates an unhappy shortened life. A split Head Line means madness.

If the Head Line is short, but the Life Line points to a long life, narrow-mindedness and intolerance are indicated. The person will hold bigoted views on certain things. He will lack imagination and will not have good judgment. His thumb and other developments will confirm this.

A thin, long and faint Head Line is treacherous. If it turns up to join the Heart Line near the end, the person's life is threatened.

When reading the Head Line, or indeed any other line, the hardness or softness of the palms should also be considered, and the Mounts should be looked at on both hands.

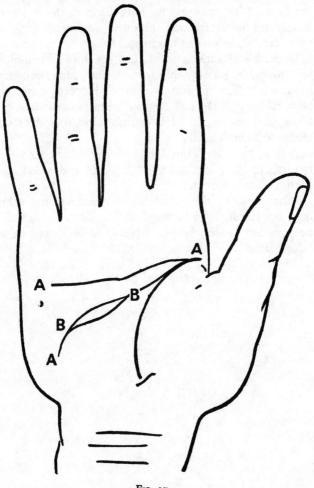

Fig. 17.

CHAPTER XI

The Life Line

THE LIFE LINE is perhaps the most interesting of all lines in the palm. Through this line it is possible to estimate the length of a person's life. I don't think it is ever possible to estimate the exact length, but it is certainly possible to come to within a very few years of it.

The length of a person's life can be estimated by comparing the length of the Life Line with that of the Fate Line.

On the Life Line the years are reckoned downwards, from the upper end, above the thumb. On the Fate Line the years are reckoned from the base of the palm upwards.

The Life Line encircles the ball of the thumb (see FIG. 9) and the health of the person can be judged by the appearance of the line. It should be clear, narrow, continuous and well-coloured, but not too red.

The first question one is usually asked is, "How long shall I live?" This question can be answered fairly accurately.

If the Life Line completely encircles the thumb, it is a sure indication that the person will live to a very old age.

The intermediate ages are more difficult to estimate, but they can be deduced fairly accurately. The way to do so is this: draw a line from the inner side of the first finger, parallel to the side of the hand, until it cuts the Life Line. This point is about 12 years of age. Continue this line to the base of the thumb, until it cuts the Life Line again. This is about 90 years of age.

The Fate Line ends on the Mount of Saturn at 90, too, near the base of the middle finger.

Half the length of the palm is about 40 years. The Fate Line cuts the Head Line at 33 to 35, according to the slope of the Head Line, and it cuts the Heart Line about 15 years later.

Of course no two hands are exactly the same, but once a date can be correctly fixed, the others follow the general rule (see FIG. 9).

Once a lady palmist read my hand and told me I was to have a fever at a certain age. Unfortunately, I was already older than the age she mentioned. But I did have the predicted attack three years later— that is, five years later than the palmist had expected it to occur.

This goes to prove my theory that it is extremely difficult to tell the exact age at which an event occurred or will occur. Palmists should be careful to look both on the Fate Line and on the Life Line when calculating the age at which an incident took place or will take place.

Sometimes, however, the age is clearly marked on the hand. I was once asked to read the hand of an old gentleman who was very sceptical about Palmistry. He had already had his hand read by two other palmists and wanted to see whether I corroborated their statements.

He asked me to tell him about the chief events in his career and this I proceeded to do.

" You went into business rather early and imme- diately took a grip of it," I told him.

" At what age? " he interrupted.

" Eighteen," I replied. " You continued in business, although you had to struggle against influences."

" What influences? " he inquired.

" Your associates—perhaps your partners. Anyway, you had a hard struggle and many worries, but you managed to stick it.

" Just after you were 45 you had your own way, made money, and I should imagine you are now entirely independent."

He asked me where I saw all this and I showed him the lines. There were interferences in his Fate Line, crosses and troubles in his Life Line, which showed his uneventful childhood, his leap into business at the age of about 18, the victory at 45 and his steady progress ever since.

" There it is. Am I right? " I asked.

" Almost entirely," he replied. " But I was 46 when I got my own way. I went into business at 18, and had a hard struggle with my partners later. But I conquered in the end. I have retired now. You are the third person to tell me these things correctly and you have all told me I first went into business at the age of 18."

" And yet you don't believe in palmistry! " I exclaimed.

" Well, no," he replied. " But I am certainly becoming interested in it."

I have said that the perfect Life Line should be clear, well coloured, of medium width and free from breaks and crosses. But of course an absolutely perfect Life Line is hardly ever seen. However, it should not be pale, broad, red, or much chained, crossed or broken.

If it is pale, broad and broken, illness is indicated.

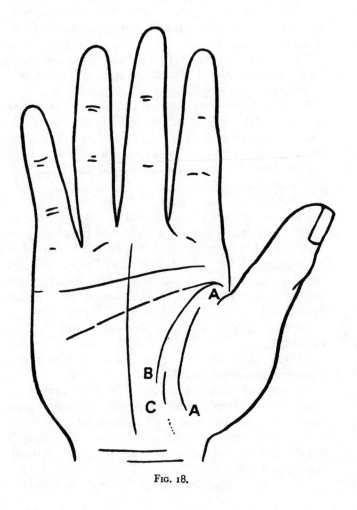

FIG. 18.

If it is pale only it means weakness both in health and character. But if, with this Life Line, the Head Line is strong, the brain will be active even if the health is poor.

A pale line points to an envious nature and if the line varies in thickness it shows an uncertain health and temper. A very red and wide Life Line is a sign of force and at times of cruelty.

Sometimes there is a line inside the Life Line, running parallel to it. This is called the Line of Mars (FIG. 18, A.A). It strengthens the Life Line and remedies the ill-effects of a broken Life Line (as in FIG. 18, B).

Forks at the beginning of the Life Line show vanity and conceit, especially if the fork is confused and broken. Forks at the end of the line show loss of money, change of work and little provision for old age, through no fault of the person himself. He may have a large family to support, he may lose money in business or his health may give way.

These signs can also be seen in the Head Line or the Heart Line. A broken Head Line and a lined Mount of Mercury sometimes indicate trouble in business. The time will be indicated by a line from the Life Line to the Head Line.

At any time the fork of the Life Line is a serious warning. Any kind of overwork should be avoided. The life breaks and may cause deep depression. At the best it means a hard ending to life. This fate is usually confirmed by a plain fork at the beginning of the line.

Sometimes dark and white spots or dots appear on the Life Line. The dark ones indicate nervous attacks (see Head Line) and the white ones affections of or injuries to the head and eyes.

The sudden ending of the line in both hands means death and small dots at the end of the line accentuate this (FIG. 18, C). The cause should be looked for in the Head and Heart Lines (see diagram) if the Life Line does not go on beyond the points.

It is a serious sign if the Life, Heart and Head Lines are joined at the beginning (FIG. 17, A). This joining of the three lines indicates a violent death and perhaps even suicide.

The Head and Life Lines *should* join clearly at the beginning. This shows a studious and careful nature (see Chapter X, on Head Line). If the lines do not join, the person may be fond of reading, but not of study, and will be careless and sometimes brusque.

Islands on the Life Line (FIG. 19, A.A) are temporary severe illnesses. The lapse of time between the illnesses can be calculated by the upright line to a spot on the Head Line which indicates the throat, etc. (FIG. 19, B.B) or to the Liver Line (FIG. 19, C.C) for other kinds of illness.

Branches which rise from the Life Line show the person's vitality. When they cut through the Head and Heart Lines, they show that success will come to the person through hard work. Descending branches mean weaknesses.

Crosses at the end of the Life Line mean failure in life, not from lack of ability but from illness, or sheer bad luck. (See also Chapter XIX.)

Lines crossing from the ball of the thumb (FIG. 19) indicate illnesses, family, head or heart worries. Trace them to their ending and find out the characteristics of the lines or Mounts where they stop. The trouble will be confirmed by stars or points at the stopping place.

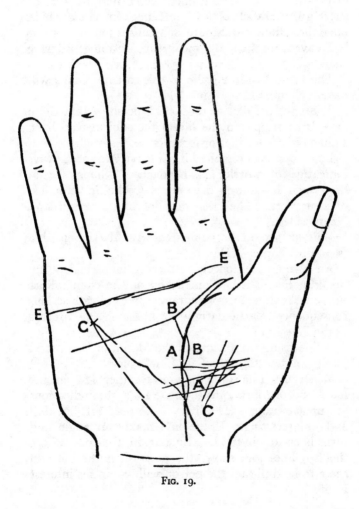

FIG. 19.

In pleasure-loving hands there are often lines which partly encircle the Mount of Venus within the limit of the Life Line. These lines, which may be long or short, run parallel to the Life Line. In hands which have these lines, the Mount of Venus is found more or less rayed, crossed by bars, thus forming a grille (FIG. 19).

The person with a grille of this sort on Venus will have a chained Heart Line (FIG. 19, E.E).

The lines parallel to the Life Line show that there have been people in the life of the subject who have influenced his feelings or fortunes.

Lines or rays across the Life Line (FIG. 19) are always indicative of worries or headaches. Some special lines, such as a cut on the Line of Apollo, indicate loss of some sort. The same applies to the Head and Heart Lines.

Illnesses should be compared with the Liver Line (see also Chapter XIV).

An island which occurs in a cross line is bad. Any break or fork is a bad omen and on the chance lines such marks show loss of character and indicate serious consequences, particularly when the same sign appears in the Fate Line.

A line rising from a star in the Mount of Venus and joining, not cutting, the Fate Line is lucky.

When the Life Line separates rather low in the hand and one fork joins the Fate Line, the indications are unfavourable. The life will be peaceful, but dull and uninteresting. If the line makes an angle and turns back to join the Life Line again, the point where the two lines join shows the date when the life will cease to be dull and the person will regain his interest in life.

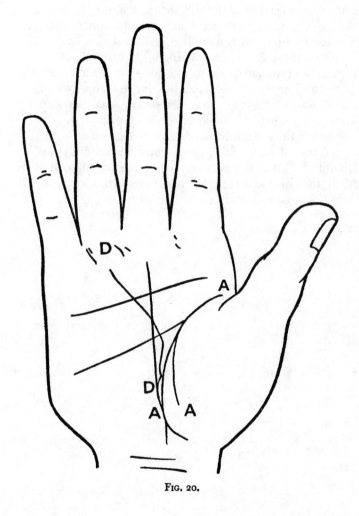

FIG. 20.

If the join occurs only in the right hand and the line continues its course in the left hand, it shows that the person has conquered the lassitude which threatened him and is mending his life.

On page 83 there is a drawing of an example of this formation (FIG. 20). You will see that a line starts from the join with the Life Line and eventually ends in Apollo. This indicates some very good luck in later life. There is, however, some danger of success not being fully realized, as Mercury sends a stop line across the Mount, which shows some inconstancy and frivolity. But if the person acts on the warning, it is likely that his good luck will come (FIG. 20, D.D).

CHAPTER XII

The Fate Line

THE FATE LINE, sometimes called the Line of Chance (FIG. 9, D.D), is another important line and it may rise from any of the four following points:

1. The Wrists or Rascettes.
2. The Life Line.
3. The Mount of the Moon.
4. The Plain of Mars.

1. When the line rises from the wrists and proceeds clearly, straight to the middle finger (not far into it) it indicates a happy and lucky life. If the line makes a deep mark on the Mount, all the better.

It is a bad sign if the line goes high into the lowest joint of the finger.

A separation or forking of the line on the Mount is a good sign. But an ascent high into the finger may be a bad sign, because Saturn is sad. In a weak hand an excess of Saturn indicates rash or criminal deeds. But if the hand is otherwise good, the high, ascending Fate Line will ensure success.

The same rules apply at the base of the hand. The line which cuts the rascettes or wrist lines is a sign of unhappiness.

2. It is a good sign when the Fate Line rises from the Life Line. A clear and well-formed Fate Line is a good thing, because it shows that its owner mixes his life and fortune. In other words, fate and life are in agreement and therefore no serious struggle against fate can upset or destroy the life. If there are no crosses

or breaks on the Fate Line, happiness is ensured and comes as a result of the person's own efforts.

It is all the better if these indications are confirmed by the Line of Apollo.

3. If the Fate Line rises clearly from the Mount of the Moon, success is indicated, but the life will be influenced by and dependent on other people. The person will be in some way led by other people. His fate is at the mercy of Luna and is often under the influence of the opposite sex. If the line ends on Jupiter there will be a happy and prosperous marriage. This is usually confirmed by a cross on Jupiter.

4. If the Fate Line rises from the Plain of Mars, it shows an uneventful or unhappy childhood and no success until late in life. When the childhood has been unhappy a faint, crossed line is often seen rising from the wrist. This also shows instability and lack of concentration.

The line which rises in the middle of the hand indicates trouble. Success will probably come to the person late in life, but it will be purely from the person's own efforts.

If the line starts clearly and straight, but fades away at the Head Line, it shows a very good beginning to life, but through the interference and influence of other people the person's career is checked. In this case the line may divide and begin again a little way away from, but parallel to, the first line, which has stopped or turned aside. This indicates a change of career.

Islands on the Fate Line are even more common than the signs of a changed career. They indicate a deep and often hopeless love for someone, and, with other signs, perhaps love for a married man or woman.

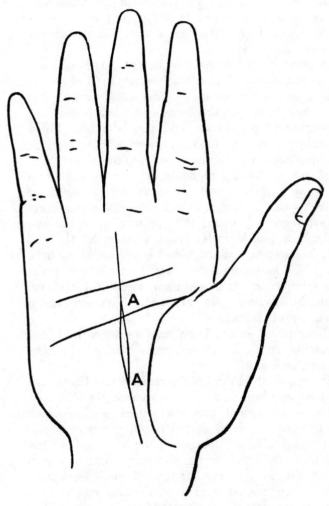

Fig. 21.

In a good hand such an attachment will bring only unhappiness. Love will be there, but the person's principles are high and so no harm will come—except his own unhappiness.

In other cases, things are different. The influence comes into the person's life at the age marked on the Fate Line when it divides. This influence may rise from the Mount of the Moon. The attachment will be confirmed by a cross and the Marriage Lines. These signs appear in some cases where marriage has been dispensed with or never even thought of.

Islands are usually found in or near the middle of the hand and are generally found on the hands of married people. If they have children, the islands are always there. The children are marked at the side of the hand (see Marriage Lines, Chapter XVI).

It is a bad sign if the island is accompanied by a star. The island must be complete to have a really strong influence. It should be a closed oval in shape, as in the diagram (FIG. 21, A.A). This indicates a strong outside influence.

Other points in the hand must be taken into consideration and will strengthen or weaken the conclusions arrived at.

Sometimes the Fate Line is clear in one hand—say the left—and broken, rayed and weak in the other.

This development shows a settled destiny which has in some way been altered (made better or worse) by the person's own doings. If the left hand is weak and the right hand strong, the person has improved his position in life. He has made himself work hard and has conquered a lazy or delicate constitution. His natural destiny was probably unimportant, but through the influence of other people and with ambi-

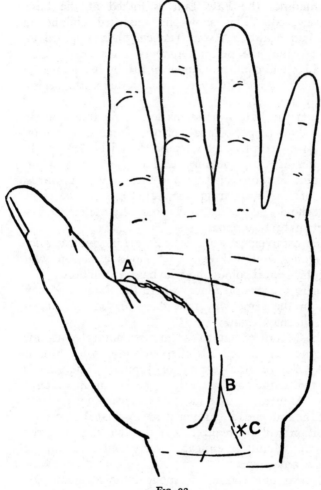

FIG. 22.

tion and will-power, he has achieved success in spite of his natural drawbacks.

Sometimes the Fate Line is forked at the base (FIG. 22, B). This shows an unsettled childhood, with bad health. A star (FIG. 22, C) is supposed to indicate that the person's parents lost money. The Life Line will confirm his poor health by being crossed and indented and, in severe cases, spotted at the beginning (FIG. 22, A).

When the Fate Line seems to stop in the hand, it shows that the person's fate or occupation has been or will be interrupted. The cause should be looked for in other lines. Sometimes the Fate Line stops in the left hand at the Head Line and then goes on upwards in a broken, wandering line. In this case the right hand should be studied to find out why the career has suddenly been stopped.

The complete absence of a Fate Line indicates an easy-going, dull existence. It shows a person who accepts life as it comes and who has no ambition.

There are several places where the Fate Line may end, in the same way that there are several places where it may begin.

The Mount of Saturn is the most natural place for the Fate Line to end. It often ends also in the Mount of Apollo, or in Mercury or Jupiter. The line is affected by the characteristic of the Mount in which it ends. Saturn will give success to a clear line.

If the line ends in Jupiter it means that the person's ambition will be realized. If the line does not rise into the Mount it indicates worry and no complete success anywhere.

A clear line ending in Apollo indicates monetary, literary or artistic success.

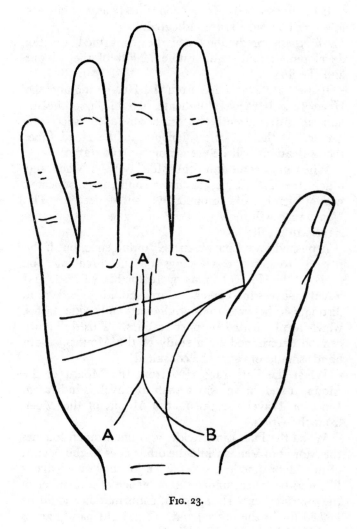

Fig. 23.

If the line ends in Mercury, business gains or success in scientific research are indicated.

All these predictions can be confirmed by the development and comparative length of the Mount and the finger.

If the Fate Line starts from the Head Line and the Head Line is weak, it indicates trouble, poor health and an intermittently but not constantly successful career. If the line rises higher than the Head Line, the indications will be even more unfavourable.

When lines come from the Mount of the Moon and touch the Fate Line, a strong influence connected with a member of the opposite sex is indicated. The Heart Line will show whether an engagement or marriage will result.

A twisted Fate Line means self-indulgence, but if the person accepts the warnings of the breaking line (beyond the Heart) he may overcome his weakness and have a successful career. Care should be taken to distinguish between self-indulgence and wide tastes, which are indicated by parting lines. This difference can be determined by a study of the Mounts. Both hands should of course be consulted.

When the Fate Line rises from the Mount of the Moon, travel, or anyway a wish to travel, is indicated. Lines of Travel rise up on the Mount of the Moon from the wrists.

When the Fate Line divides and one branch touches the Mount of Venus while the other goes to the Mount of the Moon (FIG. 23, A.A, A.B), a journey or voyage is likely to be taken, under the influence of a member of the opposite sex. Here, again, confirmation should be looked for in the other hand. The right hand carries out the indications of the left.

When the Fate Line is straight and its branches rise distinctly upwards, the indications of success are strengthened and bad luck is left behind.

Lines which cut the Fate Line mean cross influences, generally hindering ones. Their source should be carefully traced and the place where they rise should be considered.

The broken, irregular line always shows some sort of struggle, but it may be mended by other influences indicated elsewhere in the hand.

The head, the heart, imagination and will-power in the Mount of the Moon, courage in Mars and a strong Mount of Saturn will each help out a troubled Fate Line and combat the influences found there.

In these circumstances the line may change and the person's luck will be with him again.

CHAPTER XIII

The Line of Apollo

THE LINE OF APOLLO is a fairly short line which can be found beneath the third finger (FIG. 9, F.F). It can start from various places and the further down the hand the better, as success is thus ensured at an early age.

The Line of Apollo means wealth, and success in art, literature or business, according to the tendencies of the hand.

The clearer and less crossed the line is, the better will be the success or position of the person. A single line is the best of all, because then the attention is concentrated.

The usual starting places for this line are as follows:

1. From the Line of Life.
2. From the Mount of the Moon.
3. From the Plain of Mars in the Quadrangle.
4. From the Heart Line.

Each starting place gives the line a special significance.

1. A well-marked, clear Line of Apollo, starting from the Life Line, indicates that success or fame will come to the person through his own efforts. His life is devoted to his work.

2. A Line of Apollo rising from the Mount of the Moon also indicates success, but in this case it will come more through the help of other people than by the person's own unaided efforts.

3. If the Line of Apollo rises in the centre of the

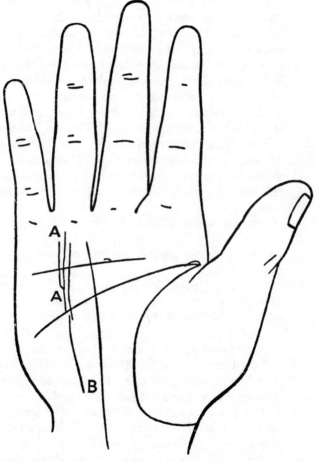

FIG. 24.

hand from the Plain of Mars, success will come to the person eventually, but only after a struggle. Mars shows this.

4. If the Line of Apollo rises from the Heart Line (late in life) the luck will come late. Even if it has not come when the person has reached middle age, it will come eventually if the line is clear and uncrossed.

Sometimes a line appears quite late beneath the little finger, from the top end of the Mount of the Moon. This indicates success which comes through another person. If this line is connected with the Head Line, the person's work will be of a literary kind.

Very often more than one line cuts the Mount of Apollo. This is not a good sign. It indicates a person whose tastes vary and who is a "Jack of all trades." He will, however, certainly appreciate art in some form.

When a broken Line of Apollo develops into a kind of star on the Mount of Apollo, it means that help will come to the person and will certainly ensure his success in life.

It is a very good sign when Jupiter (ambition) and Mercury (business sense) are both found in a hand with a good Line of Apollo. It is a sure indication of success because art and brilliancy are backed up by ambition and business talent.

The Line of Apollo should be well-coloured. A pale line is considered to be faint and therefore weak. The artistic instincts are not developed.

There are certain signs with the Line of Apollo which, when they can be seen, will affect the proper development of fortune.

For instance, a deep and hollow palm is a bad sign. Misfortune is one of the bad qualities of a hollow

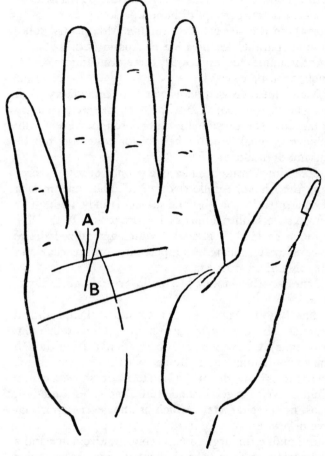

Fig. 25.

palm, and this sign is therefore an obstacle in the path of fortune.

When a twisted or crooked little finger appears with a hollow palm, it is likely that the owner will be a deceitful and perhaps dishonest person.

If there are several lines on the Mount of Apollo, running parallel to the Line of Apollo (FIG. 24, A.A), and these lines are uncrossed, there are chances of distinction in many ways.

Many lines crossed show various tendencies which have been interrupted and spoilt by poverty, jealousy or hatred. It is possible that the person may eventually achieve his goal with the help of someone else, but he will not do it alone.

Sometimes branches like two prongs of a fork come from the Line of Apollo (FIG. 25, A). Here again lack of concentration on any one subject is indicated. The person's versatility impedes his progress. If the line is much divided, a great and often unrealized desire for wealth is indicated. Opportunities may occur and they should be grasped.

Lines on the Mount of Apollo are said to indicate legacies.

The Line of Apollo gives art both in theory and in practice. If the line rises high up in the palm (FIG. 25, B) it shows a deep appreciation of art, although the person will not actually be an artist himself. If the line begins low down (FIG. 24, B) it shows artistic ability. With a good hand it also indicates a modest, unassuming character, which is, however, appreciative of praise.

In hands with large Mounts conceit, arrogance and a dictatorial manner are indicated, but in a good artistic hand Apollo is modest.

Ascending lines are always good signs.

When the Line of Apollo is well-marked, together with the development of the Mount of Venus and the Mount of the Moon, a large amount of literary ability is indicated.

If there is this development but no Mount of Venus, it is a sign of a literary critic. This type will be confirmed by short nails.

When the line only rises from the Heart Line, popularity, good nature and generosity are indicated. With this Line of Apollo there is often a hollowed hand and a divided Head Line. Success will only be fair and the person will owe his luck to his popularity and good nature.

CHAPTER XIV

The Liver or Health Line

THE LIVER LINE, or more commonly, the Health Line, rises from or near the wrist and goes upwards to the Mount of the Moon (FIG. 9, E.E). If the line is clear and unbroken it is a good sign (FIG. 26, A.A). Health and cheerfulness are indicated.

When the line rises from the base of the Life Line (FIG. 26, B.B) weakness of the lungs is indicated, especially if the Health Line is red at the join. As far as my experience goes, there is no actual heart disease, but the person will easily become short of breath after exertion. If the line is broken up indigestion is indicated.

A good Health Line is not very often seen in the hands of an adult. In youth a bad Health Line points to trouble.

Absence of a Health Line means that the person's health does not trouble him and he is vivacious, witty and quick in manner, speech and movement.

A clear Health Line indicates a good memory and business ability. If it is thick and stumpy it points to weakness in health later in life.

Crosses mean future illnesses and breaks mean past illnesses. When an illness is serious, confirmation will be found on the Life and Head Lines.

A slightly reddened Health Line is often a sign of fever in the blood. Some people say that if the redness is low down on the line, over the Life Line, a weak heart is indicated. I have only once seen this and then the only weakness was that the person became short of breath after slight exertion.

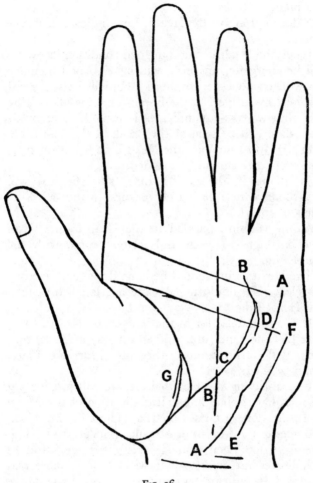

FIG. 26.

Naturally a bad Health Line points to indigestion and bilious attacks.

A deep cut across the Health Line indicates a severe illness.

When the Health Line is in good condition its owner will be energetic, unselfish, will have a good memory and will be honest in business. He will be successful and healthy in life. If the line is long, his life will be long, but a cross-cut indicates illness. The approximate date will be seen at the break in the Life Line. If this Health Line joins the Head Line it is a warning that over-work should be avoided.

An island in the Health Line (FIG. 26, C.D) will correspond with a period of weakness in the Life Line (see FIG. 26, G).

A line running parallel to the Health Line is an excellent sign. Health and fortune come with the double line.

The Health Line should be long, direct and narrow, but clear. It should not deviate nor touch the Head and Heart Lines.

It is said that a star at the base of the Health Line, near the Life Line (in a woman's hand) indicates that there will be no family. (See also Marriage Lines, Chapter XVI.)

Before leaving the Health Line, we will just look at a somewhat similar line called the Line of the Moon or Inspiration. It rises on the Mount of the Moon and goes to the Mount of Mercury (FIG. 26, E.F). This line is seldom seen, but if it is clear and straight it indicates intelligence and wit. If it is short and muddled it indicates occultism, an over-imaginative nature and perhaps even madness.

CHAPTER XV

The Girdle of Venus

THE GIRDLE OF VENUS is a semi-circular line starting from or near the base of the first finger and going on to the base of the third finger (FIG. 27, A.B). It is, in fact, a loop connecting the Mounts of Jupiter and Apollo, and including Saturn in its course.

I disagree with a statement which has often been made by writers on Palmistry to the effect that the Girdle of Venus is not often seen. I have seen this line in most hands—in the hands of men and women of high intellectual and literary merit, and cannot accept it as a sign of passion and debauchery, which many people believe it to indicate. I personally think that some of the best hands possess the Girdle of Venus. Certainly it may show a tendency to dissipation in the nature, but it must be backed up by countless other signs before the person can be condemned as being dissolute.

The Girdle of Venus really indicates a sensitive, imaginative and highly strung nature. It also indicates versatility, cleverness and smartness, which in a bad hand may become debauchery and perhaps even dishonesty.

A pale Girdle of Venus is a sign of dissipation. When the Girdle rises from the Mount of Apollo and goes downwards to the Mount of Mercury (FIG. 27, C.B) it is a very hopeful sign in a bad hand. The tendency of the Girdle to wander does not take away the love of amusement or pleasure, but it acts as a check on excessive self-indulgence.

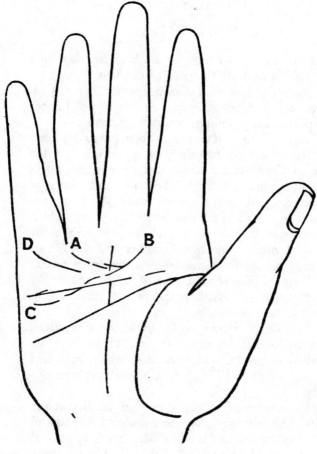

FIG. 27.

When the Girdle goes direct to Mercury, as high up on the Mount as it was on Apollo (FIG. 27, D.B), there is a strong indication of deception, because Mercury helps the liar.

THE VIA LASCIVA

There is another line, known as the Via Lasciva, which is sometimes mistaken for the Health Line. In a bad hand its appearance is only a further indication of evil.   If it is twisted it indicates cunning and fickleness.

Luckily, this line is very seldom seen and when it does appear it is usually in connection with the Head Line, which governs it.

CHAPTER XVI

Marriage and Other Lines

THE MARRIAGE LINES are deeply-cut lines which run horizontally beneath the outside of the little finger (FIG. 28, A.B). There are usually several of these lines.

If one of the lines is short and is cut by another line (FIG. 28, C) it means that the person has been engaged, but that the engagement was broken. This break will be confirmed by a line descending from the Heart Line and by a spot on the Life Line.

The way to tell when a marriage is to occur or has occurred is this: first look at the Heart and Fate Lines. There is often a line rising from the Mount of Venus, which joins the Fate Line (FIG. 28, E.F). Above the join the Fate Line divides. This strongly indicates the influence of another person and the opening up of the Heart Line shows that the heart is involved.

Now make sure that the Marriage Lines are there, and also see if there is a cross on the Mount of Jupiter (FIG. 28, H). These are the clues and the branch of the Fate Line which runs into the Heart Line gives the affection. The date of the marriage is the place on the Fate Line where it is joined by the line from the Moon, or from Venus.

Children are marked in perpendicular lines above the Marriage Lines, beneath the little finger. The deeper perpendicular lines indicate sons and the fainter, more sloping lines indicate daughters.

If the cross on the Mount of Jupiter is very near the root of the finger, the marriage will be an early one.

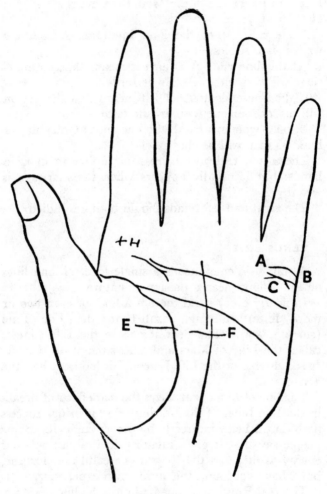

Fig. 28.

If it is in the centre of the Mount the marriage will be at 29 or 30 years.

A clear line (not the Fate Line) rising from the wrist means success.

If this line ends at Saturn it means that the marriage will be with an elderly person.

If the line ends at Apollo it means that the person will marry someone with artistic taste.

If, on a woman's hand, the line ends at Mercury, a business man will be chosen.

There is not always a cross on Jupiter in married hands, but it usually appears when the marriage is wealthy.

The right and left hands should both be studied.

VENUS LINES

A star on Venus means a single love. Many lines on the Mount mean a passionate nature.

In nearly every hand there is a line (or even two or more lines) running parallel to the Life Line (FIG. 29, A.B). The nearest one to the Life Line is called the Line of Mars and adds strength to the life. It is a double of the Life Line and is looped when the person is ill.

The line of Mars neutralizes the bad effects of breaks in the Life Line. I do not think that it brings success itself, but it helps indirectly by preventing evil. Some people say that it gives intensity to the passions and energy to life, and that it brings wealth and fortune, but I have not found this in my own experience.

The real Rings of Venus lie inside the line of Mars, nearer the thumb (FIG. 29, C.C), and indicate friendships and the influence of other people. A lucky

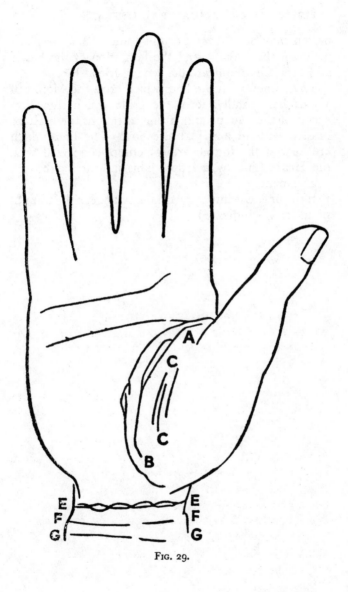

FIG. 29.

person may have several of these lines. The developments of the Mounts and the formation of the Heart and Fate Lines indicate the type of friendship.

These lines, with the lines which cross the Mount of Venus horizontally, form the grille which shows an excess of the Mount and strong affections, or perhaps passion without any real affection. The lines which are nearest the thumb are sometimes connected with the Heart Line by a loop. This indicates a broken engagement.

If the lines rise into the second phalange of the thumb, popularity is indicated.

CHAPTER XVII

The Rascettes or Bracelets

THE BRACELETS (FIG. 29, E.F.G) are lines marked fairly distinctly on the wrist, and each line is supposed to give the owner nearly thirty years of life. This measurement must be confirmed by the Life Line.

If the lines show a tendency to rise up, they indicate a person with elevated ideas, especially if they rise under the Mount of the Moon, which gives ·imagination. If they drop down under Venus, they indicate unimaginative thoughts.

If the lines are chained and interlaced near the wrist (FIG. 29, E.E) a life of hard work is indicated. The life may, however, be fairly successful.

Lines or branches from the wrists to the Mount of the Moon indicate travel, or at least a desire to travel.

Broken lines indicate struggles, losses and worries. Crosses are said to indicate legacies, but I am afraid I cannot confirm this statement. I have found crosses to indicate extravagance.

An angle in the wrist shows wealth and luck in old age.

Besides the travel lines, there are other lines rising from the wrists which cut the lower part of the Mount of the Moon. These lines indicate dangers to be feared from animals.

CHAPTER XVIII

The Quadrangle and the Triangle

THERE ARE CERTAIN SPACES in the palm which are enclosed by well-marked lines. The most important of these is the Quadrangle, which is the space between the Heart Line and the Head Line (FIG. 30, A.A). The Triangle (FIG. 30, B) is another important space. It can be seen clearly between the Life Line, the Head Line and the Health Line. Sometimes there is no Health Line. In this case the Fate Line or the Line of Apollo can be made the base of the Triangle.

THE QUADRANGLE

The Quadrangle should be regular and wide in the centre, and it should expand at both ends. This indicates good health, honesty and trustworthiness.

It is not by any means a sign of dishonesty if a person does not possess this formation, but it certainly indicates unredeeming traits such as shyness, lack of resource and fear of responsibility. The person will be too kind and generous to make a good business man. He will be very conscientious, but a little too easy-going.

This failure is the result of the person's Head and Heart Lines dipping or rising to each other, so that the square part of the Quadrangle is narrowed and the character is dwarfed.

This does not mean that the mind is narrowed; it simply means that the career will not be very successful (see Heart and Head Lines, Chapters IX and X).

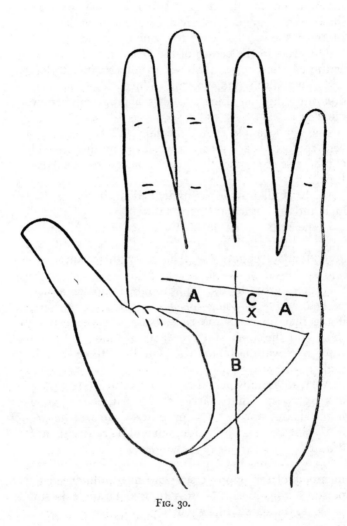

Fig. 30.

If the Quadrangle is very narrow in the centre it shows deceit and meanness. If it is extremely wide it shows extravagance. A change to width underneath Mercury shows a tendency to economy in old age.

The cross in the centre of the Quadrangle is known as the Mystic Cross. It shows an interest in astrology and spiritualism (FIG. 30, c). When the Head Line dips into the Life Line it shows a great misfortune, often in love.

The Quadrangle should be fairly clear, because a very confused space means a weakness by the descending heart-sprays and the interference with the Head Line.

If the Quadrangle is undefined it indicates bad luck and an unpleasant personality.

If the lines widen out again beneath the Mount of Apollo, the person is morally weak, but honest and kind, fond of children and liked by them, impulsive and at the same time shy.

A deep cross in the Quadrangle indicates a hen-pecked and easy-going husband. This is confirmed if the first finger of the right hand is comparatively short and the fourth finger is actually short. It indicates a chivalrous man who will be imposed on by the opposite sex.

A Head Line which rises in the centre (FIG. 31, E) indicates a shy, kind character. He will be very good-natured, but apt to break promises. He will be perfectly sincere in his intention, but will be rather scatter-brained.

Lines crossing the Quadrangle from Venus indicate members of the opposite sex who have influenced the person's affections. A cross in the Triangle is supposed to indicate a lucky journey.

Small crosses in the Quadrangle which rise and fall from the Head and Heart Lines are also influences of people of the opposite sex.

THE TRIANGLE

As I said earlier in this chapter, the Triangle is bound by the Head, Health and Life Lines (see FIG. 31).

If the Triangle is clear, well-traced and large, it indicates happiness, a good intellect and good health.

If it is wide, it indicates generosity and bravery.

If it is narrow, it indicates meanness and a dull intellect.

The three angles of the Triangle are the upper, inner and lower angles (FIG. 31, A.B.C).

1. The upper angle is formed by the Head and Life Lines. If it is a clean-cut angle, it means refinement and a good disposition. If the angle is in the Plain of Mars, it indicates an unhappy life and a mean nature.

2. The inner angle is made by the Health and Head Lines. If the angle is clear, it indicates intelligence and good health.

If it is acute, it indicates nervousness and weak health.

If the angle is obtuse, stupidity is indicated. If it is confused, it means inconstancy.

3. The lower angle, formed by the meeting of the Life and Health Lines, gives excellent health and a good character if it is acute and well-made. If the angle is too close, it indicates delicacy and a desire to make money. If it is obtuse and indistinct, it indicates laziness and a brusque manner.

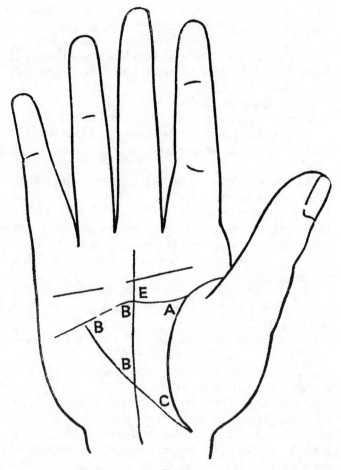

Fig. 31.

There is a smaller Triangle (FIG. 31, B.B.B) which is made by the division of the Grand Triangle, just described, by the Fate Line.   If the angles of the small Triangle are clear and well-defined, intellectual ability is indicated.   If both triangles exist the owner may well become famous.

The Triangles are worth considering, and they should confirm the deductions already arrived at by a study of the rest of the hand.

CHAPTER XIX

Signs in the Palms

I AM GOING TO DEVOTE this last chapter to descriptions and explanations of certain signs which appear in the palms, and which I have not mentioned in earlier chapters.

On all palms there can be seen crosses, stars, grilles, circles, chained lines, islands, loops, triangles, forks, spots, capillaries or bunches of little lines, waving lines, tassels at the ends of lines, sister lines, squares and so on (see FIG. 32 for details).

Each of these apparently aimless markings has a special meaning.

The hand is constantly changing in small details. As our habits and our lives change, so our palms change, and a cross of last year may become a line of hope later on. Some traits, of course, cannot be changed; they are characteristic and the marks which indicate them will remain the same.

The hand reader must always remember that a person's character cannot be judged from one line alone. The indications must be confirmed on two or more other lines before a conclusion can be reached. There must be supporting evidence, because some signs modify and neutralize others.

This means that even a bad Fate Line can be mended by a good thumb, possessing will-power and shrewdness. The Fate Line will then improve higher up in the palm, although it was broken up and indistinct in the Plain of Mars.

(1) The Cross

(2) The Star

(3) The Square

(4) The Circle

(5) The Island

(6) The Grill

(7) The Fork

(8) The Triangle

(9) The Chain

(10) The Spot or Dot

(11)

Fig. 32.

The signs which are most often to be found in the hand are the following:

THE CROSS

The cross is an unlucky sign, unless it is very clearly marked. It possesses a certain significance on the different Mounts.

Although it is a bad sign, on Jupiter it indicates marriage and the realization of our wishes. The marriage, however, may be an unhappy one.

A cross on Saturn means bad luck.

A cross on Apollo means bad luck in art or business. If the Line of Apollo is good, the cross loses its bad influence to a great extent.

A cross on Mercury indicates deception and theft.

A cross on Mars indicates an aggressive and quarrelsome nature.

A cross in the Plain of Mars means that there will be a change in the life. The cross will be connected with the Fate Line and will cut it.

A cross on the Mount of the Moon means lying.

A cross on Venus is a single love. It means one true, unselfish affection which is often unhappy, unless there is also a cross on Jupiter. Many happily married women often have a cross both on Jupiter and on Venus.

A cross at the end of the Life Line is said to indicate a change of position. I think myself that it simply indicates failing health and a consequent struggle (see Fork).

A cross on lines usually indicates some sort of change, so a person's Fate, Life and so on are affected by this mark.

THE STAR

The Star points to circumstances over which the person has no control.

On Jupiter, a star means honour and wealth.

On Saturn, a violent death is indicated, unless a square intervenes.

On Apollo, a star indicates wealth, but there will be no happiness unless the Line of Apollo is good too.

A star on Mercury indicates that the person will be discovered in theft or trickery.

A star on Mars means sudden death, perhaps in war.

On the Mount of Venus a star indicates troubles in love affairs or marriage. It is said that a star on or near the Life Line indicates law-suits.

A star on the Mount of the Moon threatens danger by water.

If there is a star at the end of the Head Line, it is a warning of weakness of the brain. A star on the Head Line near Mars is said to indicate blindness.

A star on the Fate Line is very unfortunate and the person should take great care to avoid an accident.

A star at the base of the finger of Saturn, joining the Fate Line, indicates violent death.

The appearance of a star should be carefully watched. It does not suddenly appear; it is formed gradually.

THE SQUARE

This sign is easily recognized. It protects us from accidents, from violence and from death.

A break in the Life Line enclosed in a square plainly indicates recovery from a severe illness. If the

Fate Line is bad, a square on it will save the person from his bad fate.

A square with a red tinge is said to be a sign of escape from fire.

A square certainly proves that the person has been saved from accident, death or a severe illness. It also gives common sense and coolness in danger.

THE CIRCLE

The Circle is very seldom seen. I have only seen it once myself and it proved to indicate very bad luck.

It is considered unfortunate wherever it appears, except on the Mount of Apollo, when it indicates fame.

When a circle appears on the Heart Line it indicates weakness and in the Life Line it means blindness.

THE ISLAND

The Island is usually a bad sign.

An island on the Life Line indicates illness (FIG. 33), usually of a hereditary nature.

An island on the Head Line (FIG. 33) also indicates weakness and neuralgia. Such an island, corresponding in age with an island on the Life Line, would indicate languor, depression and worry. In such circumstances the person should avoid all excitement.

An island in the Plain of Mars is said to indicate murderous tendencies, but I am afraid I cannot confirm this statement. I do think, however, that a person who has a passionate hand and an island in the Head Line would have little compunction in killing if he had to defend himself and other people.

An island in the Heart Line usually indicates some sort of emotional attachment. In a bad hand it means a wrong and unhappy attachment. In a calm and peaceful hand it indicates a very serious and real affection.

A very much looped or broken Heart Line shows a number of love affairs, engagements and flirtations. The Fate Line and the Mount of Venus confirm the signs.

An island on the Fate Line (FIG. 33) usually indicates an attachment to a married person of the opposite sex. This formation is seen in the hand of every married man and woman, so it is not necessarily a bad sign. It does, however, often point to unhappiness when it appears in the hand of an unmarried person.

THE GRILLE

The Grille is a bad sign, which emphasizes the bad qualities of the Mount on which it appears.

A grille on the Mount of Venus indicates an extremely passionate nature.

A grille on Jupiter indicates pride, a domineering nature and selfishness.

A grille on Saturn is bad luck.

A grille on Apollo indicates vanity.

A grille on Mercury indicates hypocrisy and perhaps kleptomania.

A grille on Mars points to death by violence.

A grille on the Mount of the Moon indicates discontent and sadness.

If there are no Mounts, but a grille exists where the Mount should be, a cold nature is indicated.

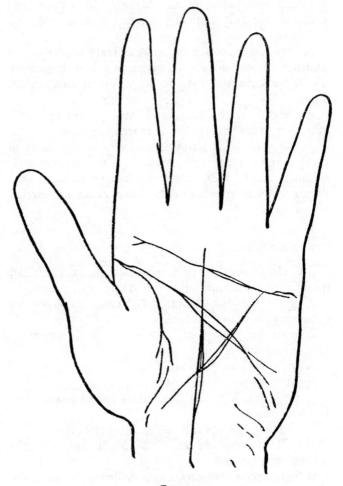

Fig. 33.

THE FORK

The parting of the lines has a certain significance.

A fork on the Head Line under Jupiter gives constancy in the affections, but unfortunately there is no happiness with the love. The person's affections are misplaced. If the fork is crossed, the love will be broken.

Upward branches or forks indicate the strength of the line. Downward forks on the Life Line show failure and loss of energy. If they form a kind of tassel, loss of money will come with the loss of health.

Branches underneath the Heart Line show disappointments in the affections. Branches above the Heart Line show happy and successful attachments. If the Heart Line has no branches, it shows a life in which there is no love for the opposite sex.

A fork on Apollo shows success in the person's chosen profession. A confused double forking indicates an attempt to do more than one thing. The efforts will end in failure because the energies are distributed and not concentrated. Parallel upright lines uncrossed by the top girdle are good and show success by hard work.

A fork in the Head Line gives imagination and common sense. A large fork indicates a deceitful nature.

The fork is usually a good sign, unless it is large and near the Head Line.

TRIANGLES, CHAINS, DOTS AND WORRY LINES

The Triangle is a sign of success in art or science. Knowledge and its application is contained in the triangle and it usually indicates success.

MELVIN POWERS SELF-IMPROVEMENT LIBRARY

ASTROLOGY

_____ ASTROLOGY: HOW TO CHART YOUR HOROSCOPE *Max Heindel*	5.00
_____ ASTROLOGY AND SEXUAL ANALYSIS *Morris C. Goodman*	5.00
_____ ASTROLOGY MADE EASY *Astarte*	3.00
_____ ASTROLOGY MADE PRACTICAL *Alexandra Kayhle*	3.00
_____ ASTROLOGY, ROMANCE, YOU AND THE STARS *Anthony Norvell*	4.00
_____ MY WORLD OF ASTROLOGY *Sydney Omarr*	7.00
_____ THOUGHT DIAL *Sydney Omarr*	4.00
_____ WHAT THE STARS REVEAL ABOUT THE MEN IN YOUR LIFE *Thelma White*	3.00

BRIDGE

_____ BRIDGE BIDDING MADE EASY *Edwin B. Kantar*	10.00
_____ BRIDGE CONVENTIONS *Edwin B. Kantar*	7.00
_____ BRIDGE HUMOR *Edwin B. Kantar*	5.00
_____ COMPETITIVE BIDDING IN MODERN BRIDGE *Edgar Kaplan*	4.00
_____ DEFENSIVE BRIDGE PLAY COMPLETE *Edwin B. Kantar*	15.00
_____ GAMESMAN BRIDGE—Play Better with Kantar *Edwin B. Kantar*	5.00
_____ HOW TO IMPROVE YOUR BRIDGE *Alfred Sheinwold*	5.00
_____ IMPROVING YOUR BIDDING SKILLS *Edwin B. Kantar*	4.00
_____ INTRODUCTION TO DECLARER'S PLAY *Edwin B. Kantar*	5.00
_____ INTRODUCTION TO DEFENDER'S PLAY *Edwin B. Kantar*	3.00
_____ KANTAR FOR THE DEFENSE *Edwin B. Kantar*	5.00
_____ KANTAR FOR THE DEFENSE VOLUME 2 *Edwin B. Kantar*	7.00
_____ SHORT CUT TO WINNING BRIDGE *Alfred Sheinwold*	3.00
_____ TEST YOUR BRIDGE PLAY *Edwin B. Kantar*	5.00
_____ VOLUME 2—TEST YOUR BRIDGE PLAY *Edwin B. Kantar*	5.00
_____ WINNING DECLARER PLAY *Dorothy Hayden Truscott*	5.00

BUSINESS, STUDY & REFERENCE

_____ CONVERSATION MADE EASY *Elliot Russell*	4.00
_____ EXAM SECRET *Dennis B. Jackson*	3.00
_____ FIX-IT BOOK *Arthur Symons*	2.00
_____ HOW TO DEVELOP A BETTER SPEAKING VOICE *M. Hellier*	4.00
_____ HOW TO SELF-PUBLISH YOUR BOOK & MAKE IT A BEST SELLER *Melvin Powers*	10.00
_____ INCREASE YOUR LEARNING POWER *Geoffrey A. Dudley*	3.00
_____ PRACTICAL GUIDE TO BETTER CONCENTRATION *Melvin Powers*	3.00
_____ PRACTICAL GUIDE TO PUBLIC SPEAKING *Maurice Forley*	5.00
_____ 7 DAYS TO FASTER READING *William S. Schaill*	3.00
_____ SONGWRITERS' RHYMING DICTIONARY *Jane Shaw Whitfield*	6.00
_____ SPELLING MADE EASY *Lester D. Basch & Dr. Milton Finkelstein*	3.00
_____ STUDENT'S GUIDE TO BETTER GRADES *J. A. Rickard*	3.00
_____ TEST YOURSELF—Find Your Hidden Talent *Jack Shafer*	3.00
_____ YOUR WILL & WHAT TO DO ABOUT IT *Attorney Samuel G. Kling*	4.00

CALLIGRAPHY

_____ ADVANCED CALLIGRAPHY *Katherine Jeffares*	7.00
_____ CALLIGRAPHER'S REFERENCE BOOK *Anne Leptich & Jacque Evans*	7.00
_____ CALLIGRAPHY—The Art of Beautiful Writing *Katherine Jeffares*	7.00
_____ CALLIGRAPHY FOR FUN & PROFIT *Anne Leptich & Jacque Evans*	7.00
_____ CALLIGRAPHY MADE EASY *Tina Serafini*	7.00

CHESS & CHECKERS

_____ BEGINNER'S GUIDE TO WINNING CHESS *Fred Reinfeld*	5.00
_____ CHESS IN TEN EASY LESSONS *Larry Evans*	5.00
_____ CHESS MADE EASY *Milton L. Hanauer*	3.00
_____ CHESS PROBLEMS FOR BEGINNERS edited by *Fred Reinfeld*	2.00
_____ CHESS SECRETS REVEALED *Fred Reinfeld*	2.00
_____ CHESS TACTICS FOR BEGINNERS edited by *Fred Reinfeld*	4.00
_____ CHESS THEORY & PRACTICE *Morry & Mitchell*	2.00
_____ HOW TO WIN AT CHECKERS *Fred Reinfeld*	3.00
_____ 1001 BRILLIANT WAYS TO CHECKMATE *Fred Reinfeld*	4.00
_____ 1001 WINNING CHESS SACRIFICES & COMBINATIONS *Fred Reinfeld*	4.00
_____ SOVIET CHESS Edited by *R. G. Wade*	3.00

COOKERY & HERBS

____ CULPEPER'S HERBAL REMEDIES *Dr. Nicholas Culpeper*   3.00
____ FAST GOURMET COOKBOOK *Poppy Cannon*   2.50
____ GINSENG The Myth & The Truth *Joseph P. Hou*   3.00
____ HEALING POWER OF HERBS *May Bethel*   4.00
____ HEALING POWER OF NATURAL FOODS *May Bethel*   5.00
____ HERB HANDBOOK *Dawn MacLeod*   3.00
____ HERBS FOR HEALTH—How to Grow & Use Them *Louise Evans Doole*   4.00
____ HOME GARDEN COOKBOOK—Delicious Natural Food Recipes *Ken Kraft*   3.00
____ MEDICAL HERBALIST *edited by Dr. J. R. Yemm*   3.00
____ VEGETABLE GARDENING FOR BEGINNERS *Hugh Wiberg*   2.00
____ VEGETABLES FOR TODAY'S GARDENS *R. Milton Carleton*   2.00
____ VEGETARIAN COOKERY *Janet Walker*   4.00
____ VEGETARIAN COOKING MADE EASY & DELECTABLE *Veronica Vezza*   3.00
____ VEGETARIAN DELIGHTS—A Happy Cookbook for Health *K. R. Mehta*   2.00
____ VEGETARIAN GOURMET COOKBOOK *Joyce McKinnel*   3.00

GAMBLING & POKER

____ ADVANCED POKER STRATEGY & WINNING PLAY *A. D. Livingston*   5.00
____ HOW TO WIN AT DICE GAMES *Skip Frey*   3.00
____ HOW TO WIN AT POKER *Terence Reese & Anthony T. Watkins*   5.00
____ WINNING AT CRAPS *Dr. Lloyd T. Commins*   4.00
____ WINNING AT GIN *Chester Wander & Cy Rice*   3.00
____ WINNING AT POKER—An Expert's Guide *John Archer*   5.00
____ WINNING AT 21—An Expert's Guide *John Archer*   5.00
____ WINNING POKER SYSTEMS *Norman Zadeh*   3.00

HEALTH

____ BEE POLLEN *Lynda Lyngheim & Jack Scagnetti*   3.00
____ DR. LINDNER'S SPECIAL WEIGHT CONTROL METHOD *P. G. Lindner, M.D.*   2.00
____ HELP YOURSELF TO BETTER SIGHT *Margaret Darst Corbett*   3.00
____ HOW TO IMPROVE YOUR VISION *Dr. Robert A. Kraskin*   3.00
____ HOW YOU CAN STOP SMOKING PERMANENTLY *Ernest Caldwell*   3.00
____ MIND OVER PLATTER *Peter G. Lindner, M.D.*   3.00
____ NATURE'S WAY TO NUTRITION & VIBRANT HEALTH *Robert J. Scrutton*   3.00
____ NEW CARBOHYDRATE DIET COUNTER *Patti Lopez-Pereira*   2.00
____ QUICK & EASY EXERCISES FOR FACIAL BEAUTY *Judy Smith-deal*   2.00
____ QUICK & EASY EXERCISES FOR FIGURE BEAUTY *Judy Smith-deal*   2.00
____ REFLEXOLOGY *Dr. Maybelle Segal*   4.00
____ REFLEXOLOGY FOR GOOD HEALTH *Anna Kaye & Don C. Matchan*   5.00
____ 30 DAYS TO BEAUTIFUL LEGS *Dr. Marc Selner*   3.00
____ YOU CAN LEARN TO RELAX *Dr. Samuel Gutwirth*   3.00
____ YOUR ALLERGY—What To Do About It *Allan Knight, M.D.*   3.00

HOBBIES

____ BEACHCOMBING FOR BEGINNERS *Norman Hickin*   2.00
____ BLACKSTONE'S MODERN CARD TRICKS *Harry Blackstone*   3.00
____ BLACKSTONE'S SECRETS OF MAGIC *Harry Blackstone*   3.00
____ COIN COLLECTING FOR BEGINNERS *Burton Hobson & Fred Reinfeld*   3.00
____ ENTERTAINING WITH ESP *Tony 'Doc' Shiels*   2.00
____ 400 FASCINATING MAGIC TRICKS YOU CAN DO *Howard Thurston*   4.00
____ HOW I TURN JUNK INTO FUN AND PROFIT *Sari*   3.00
____ HOW TO WRITE A HIT SONG & SELL IT *Tommy Boyce*   7.00
____ JUGGLING MADE EASY *Rudolf Dittrich*   3.00
____ MAGIC FOR ALL AGES *Walter Gibson*   4.00
____ MAGIC MADE EASY *Byron Wels*   2.00
____ STAMP COLLECTING FOR BEGINNERS *Burton Hobson*   3.00

HORSE PLAYERS' WINNING GUIDES

____ BETTING HORSES TO WIN *Les Conklin*   3.00
____ ELIMINATE THE LOSERS *Bob McKnight*   3.00
____ HOW TO PICK WINNING HORSES *Bob McKnight*   5.00
____ HOW TO WIN AT THE RACES *Sam (The Genius) Lewin*   5.00
____ HOW YOU CAN BEAT THE RACES *Jack Kavanagh*   5.00
____ MAKING MONEY AT THE RACES *David Barr*   5.00

_____	SEXUALLY FULFILLED MAN _Dr. Rachel Copelan_	5.00
_____	STAYING IN LOVE _Dr. Norton F. Kristy_	7.00

MELVIN POWERS' MAIL ORDER LIBRARY

_____	HOW TO GET RICH IN MAIL ORDER _Melvin Powers_	15.00
_____	HOW TO WRITE A GOOD ADVERTISEMENT _Victor O. Schwab_	15.00
_____	MAIL ORDER MADE EASY _J. Frank Brumbaugh_	10.00
_____	U.S. MAIL ORDER SHOPPER'S GUIDE _Susan Spitzer_	10.00

METAPHYSICS & OCCULT

_____	BOOK OF TALISMANS, AMULETS & ZODIACAL GEMS _William Pavitt_	5.00
_____	CONCENTRATION—A Guide to Mental Mastery _Mouni Sadhu_	5.00
_____	CRITIQUES OF GOD _Edited by Peter Angeles_	7.00
_____	EXTRA-TERRESTRIAL INTELLIGENCE—The First Encounter	6.00
_____	FORTUNE TELLING WITH CARDS _P. Foli_	4.00
_____	HANDWRITING ANALYSIS MADE EASY _John Marley_	5.00
_____	HANDWRITING TELLS _Nadya Olyanova_	7.00
_____	HOW TO INTERPRET DREAMS, OMENS & FORTUNE TELLING SIGNS _Gettings_	3.00
_____	HOW TO UNDERSTAND YOUR DREAMS _Geoffrey A. Dudley_	3.00
_____	ILLUSTRATED YOGA _William Zorn_	3.00
_____	IN DAYS OF GREAT PEACE _Mouni Sadhu_	3.00
_____	LSD—THE AGE OF MIND _Bernard Roseman_	2.00
_____	MAGICIAN—His Training and Work _W. E. Butler_	3.00
_____	MEDITATION _Mouni Sadhu_	7.00
_____	MODERN NUMEROLOGY _Morris C. Goodman_	5.00
_____	NUMEROLOGY—ITS FACTS AND SECRETS _Ariel Yvon Taylor_	3.00
_____	NUMEROLOGY MADE EASY _W. Mykian_	5.00
_____	PALMISTRY MADE EASY _Fred Gettings_	5.00
_____	PALMISTRY MADE PRACTICAL _Elizabeth Daniels Squire_	5.00
_____	PALMISTRY SECRETS REVEALED _Henry Frith_	4.00
_____	PROPHECY IN OUR TIME _Martin Ebon_	2.50
_____	PSYCHOLOGY OF HANDWRITING _Nadya Olyanova_	5.00
_____	SUPERSTITION—Are You Superstitious? _Eric Maple_	2.00
_____	TAROT _Mouni Sadhu_	8.00
_____	TAROT OF THE BOHEMIANS _Papus_	5.00
_____	WAYS TO SELF-REALIZATION _Mouni Sadhu_	3.00
_____	WHAT YOUR HANDWRITING REVEALS _Albert E. Hughes_	3.00
_____	WITCHCRAFT, MAGIC & OCCULTISM—A Fascinating History _W. B. Crow_	5.00
_____	WITCHCRAFT—THE SIXTH SENSE _Justine Glass_	5.00
_____	WORLD OF PSYCHIC RESEARCH _Hereward Carrington_	2.00

SELF-HELP & INSPIRATIONAL

_____	DAILY POWER FOR JOYFUL LIVING _Dr. Donald Curtis_	5.00
_____	DYNAMIC THINKING _Melvin Powers_	2.00
_____	GREATEST POWER IN THE UNIVERSE _U. S. Andersen_	5.00
_____	GROW RICH WHILE YOU SLEEP _Ben Sweetland_	3.00
_____	GROWTH THROUGH REASON _Albert Ellis, Ph.D._	4.00
_____	GUIDE TO PERSONAL HAPPINESS _Albert Ellis, Ph.D. & Irving Becker, Ed. D._	5.00
_____	HELPING YOURSELF WITH APPLIED PSYCHOLOGY _R. Henderson_	2.00
_____	HOW TO ATTRACT GOOD LUCK _A. H. Z. Carr_	5.00
_____	HOW TO BE GREAT _Dr. Donald Curtis_	5.00
_____	HOW TO DEVELOP A WINNING PERSONALITY _Martin Panzer_	5.00
_____	HOW TO DEVELOP AN EXCEPTIONAL MEMORY _Young & Gibson_	5.00
_____	HOW TO LIVE WITH A NEUROTIC _Albert Ellis, Ph. D._	5.00
_____	HOW TO OVERCOME YOUR FEARS _M. P. Leahy, M.D._	3.00
_____	HOW TO SUCCEED _Brian Adams_	7.00
_____	HOW YOU CAN HAVE CONFIDENCE AND POWER _Les Giblin_	5.00
_____	HUMAN PROBLEMS & HOW TO SOLVE THEM _Dr. Donald Curtis_	5.00
_____	I CAN _Ben Sweetland_	7.00
_____	I WILL _Ben Sweetland_	3.00
_____	LEFT-HANDED PEOPLE _Michael Barsley_	5.00
_____	MAGIC IN YOUR MIND _U. S. Andersen_	6.00
_____	MAGIC OF THINKING BIG _Dr. David J. Schwartz_	3.00
_____	MAGIC POWER OF YOUR MIND _Walter M. Germain_	5.00

_____ MENTAL POWER THROUGH SLEEP SUGGESTION *Melvin Powers*   3.00
_____ NEW GUIDE TO RATIONAL LIVING *Albert Ellis, Ph.D. & R. Harper, Ph.D.*   3.00
_____ PROJECT YOU *A Manual of Rational Assertiveness Training Paris & Casey*   6.00
_____ PSYCHO-CYBERNETICS *Maxwell Maltz, M.D.*   5.00
_____ SALES CYBERNETICS *Brian Adams*   7.00
_____ SCIENCE OF MIND IN DAILY LIVING *Dr. Donald Curtis*   5.00
_____ SECRET OF SECRETS *U. S. Andersen*   6.00
_____ SECRET POWER OF THE PYRAMIDS *U. S. Andersen*   5.00
_____ SELF-THERAPY FOR THE STUTTERER *Malcolm Fraser*   3.00
_____ STUTTERING AND WHAT YOU CAN DO ABOUT IT *W. Johnson, Ph.D.*   2.50
_____ SUCCESS-CYBERNETICS *U. S. Andersen*   6.00
_____ 10 DAYS TO A GREAT NEW LIFE *William E. Edwards*   3.00
_____ THINK AND GROW RICH *Napoleon Hill*   5.00
_____ THINK YOUR WAY TO SUCCESS *Dr. Lew Losoncy*   5.00
_____ THREE MAGIC WORDS *U. S. Andersen*   7.00
_____ TREASURY OF COMFORT *edited by Rabbi Sidney Greenberg*   5.00
_____ TREASURY OF THE ART OF LIVING *Sidney S. Greenberg*   5.00
_____ YOU ARE NOT THE TARGET *Laura Huxley*   5.00
_____ YOUR SUBCONSCIOUS POWER *Charles M. Simmons*   5.00
_____ YOUR THOUGHTS CAN CHANGE YOUR LIFE *Dr. Donald Curtis*   5.00

SPORTS

_____ BICYCLING FOR FUN AND GOOD HEALTH *Kenneth E. Luther*   2.00
_____ BILLIARDS—Pocket • Carom • Three Cushion *Clive Cottingham, Jr.*   5.00
_____ CAMPING-OUT 101 Ideas & Activities *Bruno Knobel*   2.00
_____ COMPLETE GUIDE TO FISHING *Vlad Evanoff*   2.00
_____ HOW TO IMPROVE YOUR RACQUETBALL *Lubarsky Kaufman & Scagnetti*   3.00
_____ HOW TO WIN AT POCKET BILLIARDS *Edward D. Knuchell*   5.00
_____ JOY OF WALKING *Jack Scagnetti*   3.00
_____ LEARNING & TEACHING SOCCER SKILLS *Eric Worthington*   3.00
_____ MOTORCYCLING FOR BEGINNERS *I. G. Edmonds*   3.00
_____ RACQUETBALL FOR WOMEN *Toni Hudson, Jack Scagnetti & Vince Rondone*   3.00
_____ RACQUETBALL MADE EASY *Steve Lubarsky, Rod Delson & Jack Scagnetti*   4.00
_____ SECRET OF BOWLING STRIKES *Dawson Taylor*   3.00
_____ SECRET OF PERFECT PUTTING *Horton Smith & Dawson Taylor*   5.00
_____ SOCCER—The Game & How to Play It *Gary Rosenthal*   3.00
_____ STARTING SOCCER *Edward F. Dolan, Jr.*   3.00

TENNIS LOVERS' LIBRARY

_____ BEGINNER'S GUIDE TO WINNING TENNIS *Helen Hull Jacobs*   2.00
_____ HOW TO BEAT BETTER TENNIS PLAYERS *Loring Fiske*   4.00
_____ HOW TO IMPROVE YOUR TENNIS—Style, Strategy & Analysis *C. Wilson*   2.00
_____ PLAY TENNIS WITH ROSEWALL *Ken Rosewall*   2.00
_____ PSYCH YOURSELF TO BETTER TENNIS *Dr. Walter A. Luszki*   2.00
_____ TENNIS FOR BEGINNERS, *Dr. H. A. Murray*   2.00
_____ TENNIS MADE EASY *Joel Brecheen*   4.00
_____ WEEKEND TENNIS—How to Have Fun & Win at the Same Time *Bill Talbert*   3.00
_____ WINNING WITH PERCENTAGE TENNIS—Smart Strategy *Jack Lowe*   2.00

WILSHIRE PET LIBRARY

_____ DOG OBEDIENCE TRAINING *Gust Kessopulos*   5.00
_____ DOG TRAINING MADE EASY & FUN *John W. Kellogg*   4.00
_____ HOW TO BRING UP YOUR PET DOG *Kurt Unkelbach*   2.00
_____ HOW TO RAISE & TRAIN YOUR PUPPY *Jeff Griffen*   5.00
_____ PIGEONS: HOW TO RAISE & TRAIN THEM *William H. Allen, Jr.*   2.00

The books listed above can be obtained from your book dealer or directly from Melvin Powers. When ordering, please remit 50¢ per book postage & handling. Send for our free illustrated catalog of self-improvement books.

Melvin Powers

12015 Sherman Road, No. Hollywood, California 91605